PELLET B Study Guide

3 Practice Tests and California POST Exam Prep
[6th Edition]

B. Hettinger

ISBN-13: 9781637987223

TABLE OF CONTENTS

ONLINE RESOURCES

We include online resources with the purchase of this study guide to help you fully prepare for the exam.

Cheat Sheet

Review the core skills you need to master the exam with easy-to-read Cheat Sheets.

Flashcards

A convenient supplement to this study guide, the flash cards enable you to review important terms easily on your computer or smartphone.

From Stress to Success

Watch "From Stress to Success," a brief but insightful video that offers the tips, tricks, and secrets experts use to score higher on the exam.

Feedback

Let us know what you think!

Access these materials at: **triviumtestprep.com/pelletb-online-resources**

Online Resources

Introduction

Congratulations on your decision to join the field of law enforcement—few other professions are so rewarding! By purchasing this book, you've already taken the first step toward succeeding in your career. The next step is to do well on the POST Entry-Level Law Enforcement Test Battery (PELLETB), which will require you to demonstrate knowledge of high school-level reading, writing, and vocabulary.

The state of California Commission on Peace Officer Standards and Training (POST) uses the PELLETB to measure test takers' writing and reading abilities and to determine the likelihood of an examinee's success in law enforcement. The exam is the gateway for admittance into the basic academy, where you will learn about police procedure and the law. The PELLETB is simply a measure of your communication skills and does not cover police procedure, which is covered at the academy.

This study guide contains a concise but comprehensive review of all of the sections tested on the PELLETB. It also includes two practice exams, each composed of approximately 78 multiple-choice questions in an effort to mimic the actual exam. Inside, you will find tips, tricks, and in-depth explanations for each testing area. The appendix contains study words related to law enforcement in order to help you improve your spelling and vocabulary skills.

Test Format and Strategies

The PELLETB consists of approximately 78 questions, all of which are multiple-choice. You will have two hours and fifteen minutes to complete the exam; this includes the time it takes to review exam instructions. As of 2025, the PELLETB will no longer include the CLOZE portion of the exam. For this reason, the test duration is shorter than it was for previous exam administrations.

PELLETB Content		
Section	**Subtests**	**Total**
Writing	Clarity (15 – 18 questions) Spelling (15 – 18 questions) Vocabulary (15 – 18 questions)	45 – 54 multiple-choice questions
Reading	Reading Comprehension (20 – 24 questions)	20 – 24 passage-based questions
Total	65 – 78 questions	2 hours 15 minutes

The test measures reading and writing aptitude over two sections: The **Writing** portion of the exam focuses on the test taker's writing abilities in the following areas:

- clarity
- vocabulary
- spelling

The **Reading** portion of the exam evaluates the test taker's reading language ability through a series of reading comprehension exercises. During this part of the exam, you will be asked to read a passage and then answer questions relating to details and information found within the passage.

Writing

The writing section of the exam is divided into three subtests. Each subtest contains between fifteen to eighteen questions as outlined below.

The **clarity subtest** evaluates your knowledge of grammar and your ability to understand how to effectively and concisely communicate ideas using the written word. The questions are presented as two sentences. You will be prompted to identify and select the sentence that is MOST clearly and correctly written. This subtest includes only the most common grammatical errors, which are discussed later in this chapter.

The **spelling subtest** evaluates the test taker's ability to spell commonly misspelled words. The questions are presented in the form of a sentence with a word missing (designated by a blank space). Keeping the sentence context in mind, you must choose the correctly spelled word from the list of answer options. This subtest does not use words from a specific list, so you should study as many common words related to law enforcement as possible. A list of words to study for this section is included in the appendix of this book.

The **vocabulary subtest** evaluates your ability to understand words commonly used in law enforcement-related documents and communications. The questions are presented as sentences with one word underlined. You will be prompted to choose the most accurate synonym or definition, given the sentence context, from the answer options.

This subtest does not use words from a specific list, so you should study as many common words related to law enforcement as possible. Lists of common prefixes, suffixes, root words, and vocabulary are provided in this book to help you study for this portion of the exam.

Reading

The reading section of the exam consists of a multiple-choice reading comprehension subtest. This section contains a total of 20 – 24 questions, all of which are based on their corresponding passages.

The **reading comprehension** subtest evaluates your ability to read and understand what is being communicated in short- and moderate-length passages (approximately 90 words each). The questions are presented after each passage in the form of "question stems" followed by several answer options. There will likely be multiple question stems (i.e., questions) related to one passage. You will be prompted to select answer options based on the information contained in the passage.

This subtest covers only common concepts. Each passage will contain all of the information needed to answer the related questions.

Tips for Tackling Multiple-Choice Questions

The following tips assume you have a basic understanding of test taking:

- how to follow test proctor instructions
- how to properly record answers

- how to ensure that the answer for the right question is recorded
- how to review an answer sheet before submitting it

If you do nothing else to prepare for this exam, be sure to learn the following quick tips. They will help you focus your efforts and to use your time wisely.

Handling Distractors

Distractors are incorrect answer options in that appear after multiple-choice questions, or stems. They are designed to "distract" you from the correct answer. For example, read and answer the question below:

Criminals are people who violate____________________.

(A) Penal Code 62
(B) civil procedure
(C) martial law
(D) criminal laws

The correct Option is D, *criminal laws*. The other, incorrect Options—the distractors—try to distract the inattentive test taker by "sounding" right or formal. While Options A and C may be partially correct—breaking a specific penal code (criminal) or martial (civilian-imposed military) law may be a crime—neither is the *best* Option. Remember: you want to select the BEST Option, even if the other options may also be correct or suitable.

Be sure to read the question for context and tone, and try to determine what is being asked. The preceding question asks for a general definition and uses wording from the question as part of the correct answer. While a criminal might violate a *specific* penal code or martial law, violations can generally be related to *any* criminal law. Because criminals are guilty of crimes and *all* criminal laws involve or pertain to crimes, option D is the *best* answer.

Develop a Time Strategy

The examination is two hours and fifteen minutes long (135 minutes). If you divide the time equally over the exam, you should have approximately one minute and forty-five seconds to answer each question. Pay attention to the time:

- Note the start and end time for each section prior to beginning the exam.
- Make a goal to complete each question in one minute or less.

One minute seems like a short amount of time, but it actually is not. You will likely complete most questions in less than thirty seconds. Develop your strategy such that you finish the easier questions quickly to allow more time to spend on the difficult questions.

Do not spend too much time on difficult questions; instead, mark them, skip them, and return to them when you have time.

Focus on the Question

Read the question carefully. Words sometimes change meaning based on context. **Context** is the part of a communication that comes before or after a specific word or passage; it provides clarity or meaning. Make sure to read and understand the question *before* selecting an answer. For example, read the following sentences:

The police **arrested** Chad when he was eighteen years old.

Chad is thirty-two years old, but his emotional development was **arrested** when he was eighteen years old.

The word *arrested* is used correctly in both sentences, but it has different meanings depending on the context. In the first sentence, *arrested* means "taken into custody"; the clue is that the sentence mentions that the action (*arrested*) was done by the police. In the second sentence, *arrested* means "to slow down or become inactive." In this sentence, the reader can make the logical conclusion that someone who is thirty-two years old but has the emotional development of an eighteen-year-old experienced a slow-down in emotional development.

Try to think of the correct answer before looking at the answer options. This strategy can prevent you from becoming distracted by the incorrect answer options and help you more easily identify the correct answer.

Correct is Not Always Best

Several answers could be correct—or close to correct—but you must choose the BEST answer option. Beware of answer options that are close to the correct answer but are merely distractions because another answer option would be better.

Use the Process of Elimination

Eliminate answer options that you know are incorrect, and choose your answer from the remaining options.

For "all of the above" and "none of the above" answer options, look for answers that include elements that break the "all" or "none" rule, such as a true element in a group of false elements or vice versa. If one element does not belong with the rest of the group's elements, then the answer cannot be "all" or "none" of the above. Reread the question and remaining answers and select the BEST answer option.

Scoring

Your raw score (the number of questions you answer correctly) will be converted into your T-score. Simply put, the **T-score** reflects how well you did against everyone else who took the test. POST provides a distribution, or a bell-shaped curve, with a midpoint, or average, of 50 and a standard deviation of 10:

- A T-score of 50 reflects average performance compared to all the other applicants who took the test.
- A T-score of 40 or below indicates a below-average performance.
- A T-score of 60 or above indicates an above-average performance.

There is no "passing" score; agencies and academies require different scores, so check with yours to determine your target T-score.

You will receive a score report that details the number of questions you answered correctly in each section. The score report will also provide your **percentile rank**, which shows how you did in comparison to other test takers. Each agency has its own entrance requirements, so be sure to check the requirements of the institutions you want to attend so you can set appropriate goals for yourself.

Administration and Test Day

The PELLETB is administered by POST-participating law enforcement agencies and academies, not by POST itself. To register for the exam, you must directly contact the participating agency or academy where you are applying. The PELLETB is a pencil-and-paper test; it is not offered as a computer-administered test, nor is it available online. You must test at a location in the state of California.

There is no penalty for guessing, so if you do not know the answer to a question, guess—you may get it right! Guesswork, however, is still a matter of deduction: eliminate as many answer options as possible before making a guess between the remaining answers.

Be sure to arrive early on test day. Check with the facility or participating agency to make sure you know what type of identification to bring (usually government-issued photo identification). Bring at least two sharpened No. 2 pencils. Personal belongings, cell phones, and other electronic, photographic, recording, or listening devices are not permitted in the testing center. Many testing centers offer lockers to secure your personal items, but you should check beforehand with the facility to be sure storage is available.

You may test only once within a thirty-day period; you may retest on the thirty-first day or later. If you retest within thirty days with a different agency, your test results will be invalidated.

For more information, visit https://post.ca.gov/LE-Entry-Level-Test-Battery-Applicant-FAQs.

About Trivium Test Prep

Trivium Test Prep uses industry professionals with decades' worth of knowledge in their fields, proven with degrees and honors in law, medicine, business, education, the military, and more, to produce high-quality test prep books for students.

Our study guides are specifically designed to increase any student's score. Our books are also shorter and more concise than typical study guides, so you can increase your score while significantly decreasing your study time.

How to Use This Guide

This guide is not meant to waste your time on superfluous information or concepts you've already learned; instead, we hope that you will use this guide to focus on the concepts *you* need to master for the test as well as to develop critical test-taking skills. To support this effort, the guide provides the following features:

- organized concepts with detailed explanations
- practice questions with worked-through solutions
- key test-taking strategies
- tips, tricks, and test secrets

Because we have eliminated filler and fluff, you'll be able to work through the guide at a significantly faster pace than you would with other study guides. By allowing you to focus only on those concepts that will increase your score, we'll help make your study time shorter and more effective.

The chapters in this book are divided into a review of the topics covered on the exam. This book is not intended to teach you everything you'll see on the test: there is no way to cram all of that material into one book! Instead, we are going to help you recall information that you've already learned, and—more importantly—we'll show you how to apply that knowledge. Each chapter includes an extensive review with practice questions to test your knowledge. With time, practice, and determination, you'll be well prepared for exam day.

Writing

Written and verbal communications are equally important in law enforcement. Writing accurate, clear, and concise memos, warrants, and police reports ensures that the information provided is as the officer intended. Unclear or confusing verbal communication can create misunderstanding and even danger if an officer is attempting to control a volatile situation. The same is true of written work. Wordy, incoherent, error-laden communications create confusion. The PELLETB therefore specifically tests three aspects of writing: clarity, vocabulary, and spelling.

Clear and concise writing helps readers easily understand a message. In law enforcement, the last thing an officer wants is for lawyers, juries, or the public to have to *guess* what he or she meant in a report or other written communication. **Cases have been won—and lost—based on officer testimony related to a well-written or poorly written report.**

Inspect the following two passages as an example of how wordiness and grammatical errors can confuse communication.

Passage One

On Friday, August 17, 2014, about 1530 hours while working as a patrol officer in full uniform in Sector 2 of River City I heard over my car radio that Officer Smith had two people in front of Superior Court with warrants. I arrived at the Superior Court and met with Officer Smith. Officer Smith told me a woman, identified as Jane Johnson, and a man, identified as Ronald Jones, were at the courthouse. Jane and Ronald were at the court for a family hearing.

A records check with River City Records and Warrants confirmed Jane had a misdemeanor warrant, and Ronald had a felony warrant, out of River City.

Jane and Ronald were arrested without incident to answer for the warrant.

Passage Two

On Friday, August 17, 2014, about 1530 hours I contacted Jane Johnson and Ronald Jones in front of the River City Superior Court. Jane and Ronald were at the court for a family hearing. I had information both parties had active warrants for their arrests.

A records check with River City Records and Warrants confirmed Jane had an active misdemeanor warrant for her arrest and Ronald had an active felony warrant for his arrest, both issued by River City.

I arrested Jane and Ronald without incident to answer for their warrants.

Passage two is written with sentences clear, concise, and grammatically correct; the sentences also contain all of the necessary information. Passage one, on the other hand, is wordy and filled with grammatical errors, making it unclear. Unclear or confusing reports of search warrants could result in poor investigations, arrests, and prosecutions.

The Clarity subsection of the PELLETB tests only common grammatical mistakes and requires the test taker to identify the MOST clearly written of two sentences. Knowing the rules of grammar, mechanics, and sentence structure will help you identify the correct answer on the PELLETB. Furthermore, avoiding common errors can help add clarity to your written communication. This chapter will provide a review of the basics of clear writing as well as common mistakes.

The other two exam subsections—Vocabulary and Spelling—require you to define and spell words. This chapter therefore also features information to help you build your vocabulary, determine the meanings of unfamiliar words, and review basic spelling rules.

The Parts of Speech

Nouns are the words that describe people, places, things, and ideas. The subject of a sentence is typically a noun. For example, in the sentence "The station was very clean," the subject, *station*, is a noun because it is a place. Nouns have several subcategories:

- **common nouns** (*chair, car, house*)
- **proper nouns** (*Julie, David*)
- **noncountable nouns** (*money, water*)
- **countable nouns** (*dollars, cubes*)

There is much crossover among these subcategories. For example, *chair* is both a common noun and a countable noun). Other subcategories of nouns also exist, such as pronouns and, in some cases, antecedents:

- **Pronouns** replace nouns in a sentence or paragraph, allowing a writer to achieve a smooth flow throughout a text by avoiding unnecessary repetition.
- The word the pronoun replaces is called its **antecedent**.
    - For example, in the sentence "Ruby saw Sally and waved to her," *Sally* is the antecedent of the pronoun *her.*

While there are countless nouns in the English language, there are only a few types of pronouns, the most common of which are singular and plural pronouns (Table 1.1.). For example, let's look at the following sentence:

Sam stayed home from school because Sam was not feeling well.

The noun *Sam* appears twice in the same sentence; instead, the pronoun *he* can be used to stand in for *Sam*:

Sam stayed home from school because he was not feeling well.

When using pronouns, it is important to ensure clarity as to which antecedent a pronoun is referring; this is a concept that will likely be included on the exam. When the reader cannot determine who or what a pronoun is referring to, it means that the sentence is unclear. This can happen when there are more than two nouns in a sentence; in such instances, sentences should be rewritten in order to avoid confusion:

The officer apprehended the suspect when she arrived at the home.

In the sentence above, it is unclear to whom the pronoun *she* is referring: is it referring to the officer or the suspect?

By slightly revising this sentence, it is now clear that the pronoun *she* is referring to the officer—not the suspect.

When the officer arrived at the home, she apprehended the suspect.

Table 1.1. Singular and Plural Pronouns	
Singular Pronouns	**Plural Pronouns**
▪ I, me, my, mine ▪ you, your, yours ▪ he, him, his ▪ she, her, hers ▪ it, its	▪ we, us, our, ours ▪ they, them, their, theirs

Verbs express action (*run, jump, play*) or state of being (*is, seems*). Verbs that describe action are **action verbs**, and those that describe being are **linking verbs:**

- **Action:** My brother plays tennis.
- **Linking:** He is the best player on the team.

Adjectives provide more information about a noun in a sentence. Take the following sentence:

The boy hit the ball.

If you want your readers to know more about the noun *boy*, you could use an adjective to describe him:

- *the little boy*
- *the young boy*
- *the tall boy*

Adverbs describe verbs, adjectives, and even other adverbs. The adverb *recently* in the following sentence tells us more about how the action *hired* took place:

The doctor had recently hired a new employee.

Participles are nouns or adjectives that are formed by adding *–ed* or *–ing* to a verb:

Seated politely, Ron listened to his friend's boring story.

Maya admired the sleeping cat.

Prepositions express the location of a noun or pronoun in relation to other words and phrases described in a sentence:

The nurse parked her car in a parking garage.

In the sentence above, the preposition *in* describes the position of the car in relation to the garage. Together, the preposition and the noun that follow it are called a **prepositional phrase**. In the above example, the prepositional phrase is *in a parking garage*.

Conjunctions connect words, phrases, and clauses. **Interjections**, like *wow* and *hey*, express emotion and are most commonly used in conversation and casual writing.

Practice Questions

1. Which answer option contains all of the nouns used in the following sentence?

I have lived in Minnesota since August, but I still don't own a warm coat or gloves.

(A) coat, gloves
(B) I, coat, gloves
(C) Minnesota, August, coat, gloves
(D) I, Minnesota, August, warm, coat, gloves

2. Which answer option contains all of the adjectives in the following sentence?

The new chef carefully stirred the boiling soup and then lowered the heat.

(A) new, boiling
(B) new, carefully, boiling
(C) new, carefully, boiling, heat
(D) new, carefully, boiling, lowered, heat

3. Choose the word that best completes the following sentence.

Her love ______ blueberry muffins kept her coming back to the bakery every week.

(A) to
(B) with
(C) of
(D) about

Punctuation

The basic rules for using the major punctuation marks are provided in Table 1.2.

Table 1.2. Using Punctuation

Punctuation	Purpose	Example
Period	ending sentences	Periods go at the end of complete sentences.
Question mark	ending questions	What's the best way to end a sentence?
Exclamation point	ending sentences that show extreme emotion	I'll never understand how to use commas!
Comma	joining two independent clauses (always with a coordinating conjunction) setting apart introductory and nonessential words and phrases separating items in a list	Commas can be used to join clauses, but they must always be followed by a coordinating conjunction. Commas, when used properly, set apart extra information in a sentence.

Table 1.2. Using Punctuation		
Punctuation	**Purpose**	**Example**
		My favorite punctuation marks include the colon, semicolon, and period.
Semicolon	joining together two independent clauses (never used with a conjunction)	I love exclamation points; they make sentences seem so exciting!
Colon	introducing a list, explanation, or definition	When I see a colon, I know what to expect: more information.
Apostrophe	forming contractions showing possession	It's amazing how many people can't use apostrophes correctly. Apostrophes are my sister's favorite punctuation; she finds commas' rules confusing.

Be on the lookout for **comma splices**, which describe when two independent clauses are joined by a comma WITHOUT a coordinating conjunction:

Incorrect: *Two patrol units arrived on scene, only one unit stayed.*

Correct: *Two patrol units arrived in scene, but only one unit stayed.*

Practice Questions

4. Which one of the following sentences contains an error in punctuation?
   (A) I love apple pie! John exclaimed with a smile.
   (B) Jennifer loves Adam's new haircut.
   (C) Billy went to the store; he bought bread, milk, and cheese.
   (D) Alexandra hates raisins, but she loves chocolate chips.

5. Which punctuation mark correctly completes the sentence?

*Sam, do you want to come with us for dinner*___
   (A) .
   (B) ?
   (C) ;
   (D) :

Phrases

Understanding subjects and predicates is key to understanding what phrases are:

- The **subject** is what the sentence is about.
- The **predicate** contains the verb and its modifiers.

The nurse at the front desk will answer any questions you have.

Subject: *the nurse at the front desk*

Predicate: *will answer any questions you have*

A **phrase** is a group of words that communicates only part of an idea because it lacks either a subject or a predicate. Phrases can begin with prepositions, verbs, nouns, or participles:

- **Prepositional phrase:** The dog is hiding under the porch.
- **Verb phrase:** The chef wanted to cook a different dish.
- **Noun phrase:** The big red barn rests beside the vacant chicken house.
- **Participial phrase:** Walking quietly, she tried not to wake the baby.

Practice Question

Identify the type of phrase underlined in the following sentence:

6. The experienced paraprofessional worked independently with the eager students.
   (A) prepositional phrase
   (B) noun phrase
   (C) verb phrase
   (D) participial phrase

Clauses

Clauses contain both a subject and a predicate. They can be either independent or dependent:

- An **independent** (or **main**) **clause** can stand alone as its own sentence:

The dog ate the girl's homework.

- **Dependent** (or **subordinate**) **clauses** cannot stand alone as their own sentences. They start with a subordinating conjunction, relative pronoun, or relative adjective, which will make them sound incomplete.

Because the dog ate her homework

Clauses can be joined together to create more complex sentences:

- **Coordinating conjunctions** join two independent clauses.
- **Subordinating conjunctions** join an independent clause to a dependent clause.

Table 1.3. Conjunctions		
Coordinating	*for, and, nor, but, or, yet, so* (FANBOYS)	The nurse prepared the patient for surgery, and the doctor performed it.
Subordinating	*after, although, because, if, since, so that, though, until, when, while*	She had to ride the subway because her car was being serviced.

Practice Question

Choose the word that best completes the sentence.

7. Christine left her house early on Monday morning, ___ she was still late for work.
   (A) but
   (B) and
   (C) for
   (D) or

Common Grammatical Errors

Pronoun-Antecedent Agreement

In addition to ensuring that pronoun usage will allow the reader to understand exactly to whom or what the pronoun is referring (as discussed earlier), pronouns must also agree in number with their **antecedents** (the words they replace); however, some pronouns also require gender agreements (*him, her*). **Pronoun-antecedent agreement** rules are as follows:

- Antecedents joined by *and* typically require a plural pronoun.

The children and their dogs enjoyed their day at the beach.

- If the two nouns refer to the same person, a singular pronoun is preferable.

My best friend and confidant still lives in her log cabin.

- For compound antecedents joined by *or*, the pronoun agrees with the nearer or nearest antecedent.

Either the resident mice or the manager's cat gets itself a meal of good leftovers.

- When indefinite pronouns function in a sentence, the pronoun must agree with the number of the indefinite pronoun.

Neither student finished his or her assignment.

Both students finished their assignments.

- When collective nouns function as antecedents, the pronoun choice will be singular or plural depending on the function of the collective.

The audience was cheering as it rose to its feet in unison.

Our family are spending their vacations in Maine, Hawaii, and Rome.

- When the words *each* and *every* precede the antecedent, the pronoun agreement will be singular.

Each and every man, woman, and child brings unique qualities to his or her family.

Every creative writer, technical writer, and research writer is attending his or her assigned lecture.

Let's review: how would you complete the following sentence?

Every boy and girl should check ____homework before turning it in.

Many people would use the pronoun *their*. But since the antecedent is "every boy and girl," the correct answer would technically be *his or her*; however, using *they* or *their* in similar situations is increasingly accepted in formal speech. It is unlikely that you will see questions like this on the PELLETB, but if you do, it is safest to use the technically correct response, which in this case is *his or her*.

Practice Questions

8. In which of the following sentences do the nouns and pronouns NOT agree?
   (A) After we walked inside, we took off our hats and shoes and hung them in the closet.
   (B) The members of the band should leave her instruments in the rehearsal room.
   (C) The custodian on duty should rinse out his or her mop before leaving for the day.
   (D) When you see someone in trouble, you should always try to help them.

Vague or Unclear Pronouns

A vague or unclear reference is generally the result of a **pronoun error**. Pronoun errors occur when it is not clear what the antecedent of a pronoun is (i.e., the word the pronoun replaces). In the first sentence below, it is difficult to determine whose notes the officer gave to the Assistant District Attorney (ADA): do the notes belong to the officer or to the ADA? The antecedent of the pronoun *his* is unclear. To improve this sentence, be sure the pronoun refers to only one antecedent noun.

Incorrect: *Officer Lane gave Assistant District Attorney Poole his notes.*

Correct: *Officer Lane gave his notes to Assistant District Attorney.*

Another way to ensure clarity in writing is to avoid using pronouns to refer to an implied idea; it is better to state the idea explicitly. In the sentence below, the writer misuses the pronoun *it*. The reader might be confused: did jury deliberation take a long time, or did the process of the trial take a long time? To improve this sentence, the writer should state the idea explicitly and avoid using a pronoun altogether.

Incorrect: The jury reached a verdict in the defendant's case, but it took a long time.

Correct: The jury reached a verdict in the defendant's case, but the deliberations took a long time.

Practice Question

9. Choose the more clearly written sentence.
   (A) John said he and Frank were fighting when he was shot.
   (B) John said he and Frank were fighting when Frank was shot.

Subject-Verb Agreement

Verbs are conjugated to indicate **person**, which refers to the point of view of the sentence:

- **First-person** point of view is the speaker (*I, we*).
- **Second-person** point of view is the person being addressed (*you*).
- **Third-person** point of view is outside the conversation (*they, them*).

Verbs are also conjugated to match the **number** (singular or plural) of their subjects. **Helping verbs** (*to be, to have, to do*) are used to conjugate verbs. An unconjugated verb is called an **infinitive** and includes the word *to* in front of it (*to be, to break*).

Table 1.4. Verb Conjugation (Present Tense)		
Person	**Singular**	**Plural**
First-person	*I* give	*we* give
Second-person	*you* give	*you* (all) give
Third-person	*he/she/it* gives	*they* give

Verbs must agree in number with their subjects. (In some other languages, such as Spanish, verbs must also agree in gender with their subjects.) **Subject-verb agreement** rules follow:

- Singular subjects agree with singular verbs; plural subjects agree with plural verbs.

The girl walks her dog. The girls walk their dogs.

- Compound subjects joined by *and* typically take a plural verb unless they are considered one item.

Correctness and precision are required for all good writing.

Macaroni and cheese makes a great treat for children.

- Compound subjects joined by *or* or *nor* agree with the nearer or nearest subject.

Neither I nor my friends are looking forward to our final exams.

Neither my friends nor I am looking forward to our final exams.

- All singular indefinite pronouns agree with singular verbs.

Neither of the students is happy about the play.

Each of the many cars is on the grass.

Every one of the administrators speaks highly of Officer Larkin.

- All plural indefinite pronouns agree with plural verbs.

Several of the students are happy about the play.

Both of the cars are on the grass.

Many of the administrators speak highly of Officer Larkin.

- Some of the singular indefinite pronouns (*all, most, some, more, any*) change agreement depending on the object of the preposition.

All of the pie is gone.

All of the pies are gone.

Some of the bucket is dirty.

Some of the buckets are dirty.

- Collective nouns agree with singular verbs when the collective acts as one unit. Collective nouns agree with plural verbs when the collective acts as individuals within the group.

The jury announces its decision after sequestration. (They act as one unit.)

The jury make phone calls during their break time. (They act as individuals.)

- Nouns that are plural in form but singular in meaning will agree with singular verbs.

Measles is a painful disease.

Sixty dollars is too much to pay for that book.

- Singular verbs come after titles, business corporations, and words used as terms.

"Three Little Kittens" is a favorite nursery rhyme for many children.

General Motors is a major employer for the city.

Practice Question

10. Which one of the following sentences contains a subject-verb error?
    (A) The witness and her mother are asked to remain seated.
    (B) Some of the officers at the station is planning to stay late.
    (C) My partner and I are happy with the new schedule.
    (D) The department is hiring for many new positions this year.

Verb Tense Agreement

Verbs are also conjugated to indicate **tense**, or when the action has happened. Actions can happen in the past, present, or future. Tense also describes over how long of a period an action took place:

- **Simple** verbs describe general truths or something that happened once.
- **Continuous** verbs describe an ongoing action.
- **Perfect** verbs describe repeated actions or actions that started in the past and have been completed.
- **Perfect continuous** verbs describe actions that started in the past and are continuing.

Table 1.5. Verb Tenses

Tense	PAST	PRESENT	FUTURE
Simple	*I gave her a gift yesterday.*	*I give her a gift every day.*	*I will give her a gift on her birthday*
Continuous	*I was giving her a gift when you got here.*	*I am giving her a gift; come in!*	*I will be giving her a gift at dinner.*
Perfect	*I had given her a gift before you got there.*	*I have given her a gift already.*	*I will have given her a gift by midnight.*

Table 1.5. Verb Tenses			
Tense	**PAST**	**PRESENT**	**FUTURE**
Perfect continuous	*Her friends had been giving her gifts all night when I arrived.*	*I have been giving her gifts every year for nine years.*	*I will have been giving her gifts on holidays for ten years next year.*

The verb tenses in a sentence must agree with each other and with the other information provided in the sentence. Pay attention to words like *before, after, tomorrow, yesterday, then,* and *next*, which describe when in time events occurred:

Incorrect: *After he changed clothes, the officer will be ready to go home.*

Correct: *After he changed clothes, the officer was ready to go home.*

In the example above, the introductory phrase describes an action that was completed in the past (*he changed*), so the rest of the sentence should also be in the past (*was ready*).

Practice Question

11. Which verb phrase best completes the sentence?

By this time tomorrow, we ____ in New York.

(A) will have arrived
(B) have arrived
(C) arrive
(D) was arriving

Comparing Adjectives and Adverbs

The suffix *–er* is used when comparing two things, and the suffix *–est* is used when comparing more than two things. Adjectives longer than two syllables are compared using *more* (for two things) or *most* (for three or more things):

Anne is taller than Steve, but Steve is more coordinated.

Of the five brothers, Billy is the funniest, and Alex is the most intelligent.

The words *more* and *most* should NOT be used in conjunction with *–er* and *–est* endings.

Incorrect: My most warmest sweater is made of wool.

Correct: My warmest sweater is made of wool.

Practice Question

12. Which of the following sentences contains an adjective error?

(A) The new red car was faster than the old blue car.
(B) Reggie's apartment is in the tallest building on the block.
(C) The slice of cake was tastier than the brownie.
(D) Of the four speeches, Jerry's was the most long.

Misplaced Modifiers

A **modifier** is a word or phrase—like an adjective—that adds detail to a sentence. Adjectives, adverbs, and modifying phrases should be placed as close as possible to the words they modify. **Misplaced modifiers** can create confusing or nonsensical sentences:

Incorrect: *Running down the alley, the siren sounded and the police officer knew backup had arrived.*

Correct: *Running down the alley, the police officer heard the siren and knew backup had arrived.*

In the first example above, the phrase *running down the alley* looks like it is modifying *the siren*. For clarity, it should be placed next to *the police officer*, the noun it is modifying.

Incorrect: *Describing the crime, the jury listened to the prosecutor deliver his opening statement.*

Correct: *The jury listened to the prosecutor deliver his opening statement describing the crime.*

In this example, the phrase *describing the crime* is first placed next to the word *jury*, making it seem like the jury is describing the crime. To fix the sentence, the modifier should be moved so that it is clear that the prosecutor is describing the crime.

Practice Questions

13. Choose the more clearly written sentence.
    (A) During police contacts, failure to follow directions is often the cause of officer uses of force.
    (B) During police contacts, failure to follow directions often is the cause of officer uses of force.

Sentence Fragments

A **sentence fragment** occurs when a group of words is followed by a period but does not form a complete sentence or thought. A sentence fragment can be corrected by turning it into a complete sentence that has at least one independent clause:

Incorrect: *Because he was tired of presiding over cases involving the same criminals in his courtroom.*

Correct: *The judge left the bench because he was tired of presiding over cases involving the same criminals in his courtroom.*

Practice Question

14. Choose the more clearly written sentence.
    (A) The suspect robbed an elderly woman and then fled the scene in a red sedan heading northbound on Eighth Avenue.
    (B) The suspect robbed an elderly woman and then fled the scene in a red sedan. Heading northbound on Eighth Avenue.

Run-on Sentences

A **run-on sentence** describes two or more complete sentences that are not separated by appropriate punctuation (e.g., a comma, period, or semicolon), as seen in the following example:

Jack shot his friend Mark over a pool game, Jack was mad because he thought Mark was cheating.

To avoid creating run-on sentences, be sure to separate each complete thought with proper punctuation. For example, applying this rule changes the preceding sentence as follows:

Jack shot his friend Mark over a pool game. Jack was mad because he thought Mark was cheating.

Practice Question

15. Choose the more clearly written sentence.
    (A) Jane broke into the house intending to steal items to exchange for drugs she activated the alarm and ran away.
    (B) Jane broke into the house intending to steal items to exchange for drugs. She activated the alarm and ran away.

Vocabulary

Vocabulary describes a collection of words that are used or known in language. Possessing a large vocabulary can help you better understand communications by improving your ability to determine context and add clarity to the written or spoken word.

Although law enforcement vocabulary can be very technical, it contains many commonly used words. The vocabulary section of the PELLETB measures your ability to understand and appropriately use these common words.

On the PELLETB, each question is structured as one sentence with a word underlined. The answer options list alternative words to replace the underlined word. You must choose the word that MOST CLOSELY matches the meaning of the underlined word. Developing a large vocabulary takes time and practice and cannot be done overnight; however, studying commonly used words and their synonyms can help.

Synonyms are words that share the same—or nearly the same—meaning as other words. Understanding word roots, prefixes, suffixes, and how they affect words can help you determine the meaning of unfamiliar words based on how the words are structured.

Root Words

A **root word** is the base of a word. It comes after a prefix or before a suffix. In English, many root words come from ancient Greek and Latin. Root words hold meaning and can stand alone as words. Learning to recognize common root words can help you build your vocabulary and make educated guesses about unfamiliar words; it can also help improve your ability to comprehend various types of communications. Table 1.6. lists some common root words, their meanings, and examples.

Table 1.6. Common Root Words		
Root	**Meaning**	**Examples**
actus, act	drive, lead, act	active, action, activate, react
acurer	to sharpen	acute, acumen, acuity
agon	contest, struggle	antagonist, agony
ambi	both	ambiguous, ambidextrous
anthropo	man, human, humanity	anthropologist, philanthropist
aqua	water	aquarium, aquatic
arbit	judge	arbitrary, arbitration
archos, arch	chief, first, rule	monarch, archangel, anarchy
aud	to hear	audience, audible, auditory
auto	self	autobiography, autograph, autoimmune, automobile
bene	good	benevolent, beneficial
bio	life	biology, biography
capere, cip, cept	take, seize	captive, capture, captivate, intercept
cedere, ced	to go, yield	recede, precede, exceed, predecessor
chron	time	chronological, chronic, synchronize
circum	around	circumference, circumvent, circumscribe
clino, clin	lean, slant	incline, decline, inclination, recline
contra, counter	against	contradict, contrary, counteract
cred	believe	creed, incredible
crit	judge	criticize, critical

Table 1.6. Common Root Words

Root	Meaning	Examples
crypto, crypt	hide, conceal	cryptic, cryptogram, encryption
dict	to say	dictation, dictate, predict
duc, duct	to lead	conduct, induce, induct
dyna	power	dynamic, dynamite, dynamo
dys	bad, hard, unlucky	dysfunctional, dyslexic, dystopia
equ	equal, even	equidistant, inequity, equivalent, equitable
errare, err, errat	wander, go astray	errant, err, erratic, aberration
fac	to do, to make	factory, manufacture, artifact
finis, fin	end, limit	final, definite, infinite
form	shape	conform, reform
fort	strength	fortitude, fortress, fortify, comfort
fract	to break	fracture, fraction
gno, gnos	know	diagnosis, ignore, incognito, cognitive
gram	something written	telegram, diagram, grammar
graph	writing	graphic, autograph
gravis, grav, griev	heavy, serious	grave, grievance, grievous, aggravate, gravity
hetero	different	heteronym, heterogeneous
homo	same	homonym, homogenous
hydro	water	hydrate, dehydrate, hydraulic
hypo	below, beneath	hypothermia, hypothetical, hypoglycemic
ject	throw	eject, project, reject

Table 1.6. Common Root Words		
Root	**Meaning**	**Examples**
jud	judge	judicial, prejudice
jus, jur, just	right, law, oath	abjure, perjury, conjure, jury, jurisprudence
juven	young	juvenile, rejuvenate
mal	bad	malfeasance, malevolent, malcontent
mater	mother	maternal, maternity
meter, metr	measure	thermometer, perimeter, metric
micro	small	microbe, microscope, microchip
mis, miso	hate, wrong	misanthrope, misogyny, misbehave
mono	one	monologue, monotonous, monotheism
morph	form, shape	morphology, metamorphosis
mort	death	mortal, mortician, immortal
multi	many	multimedia, multiple, multiply, multicolored
nym	name	antonym, synonym, homonym
onus, oner	burden	onerous, onus, exonerate
opsis, optic	sight, eye, view	optical, synopsis
pater	father	paternal, paternity
phil	love	philanthropist, philosophy
phobia	fear	claustrophobia, acrophobia, phobic
phon	sound	cacophony, phonetic, symphony

Table 1.6. Common Root Words		
Root	**Meaning**	**Examples**
photo, phos	light	photograph, photogenic, phosphorous
placo	appease	placate, placid
port	to carry	portable, transportation, export
pretiare, prec	to value	precious, deprecation, depreciation, appreciation
pseudo	false	pseudonym, pseudoscience
psycho	soul, spirit	psychology, psychic, psychotic
rupt	to break	bankrupt, disrupt, erupt
scope	to watch, see	microscope, telescope
scrib, scribe	to write	inscribe, prescribe, describe
sect, sec	to cut	bisect, section, intersect, dissect
sentire, sent	to feel, perceive	consent, resent, sentient, sentiment
skep, scop	examine	skeptical, scope
spect	to look	inspect, spectator, circumspect, retrospective
struct	to build	construct, destruct, restructure, infrastructure
tacere, tac, tic	to be silent	tacit, taciturn, reticent
techno	art, science, skill	technique, technology
tele	far off	television, telephone, teleport
tendere	stretch	extend, tend, distend
terrere, terr	frighten	deter, terror, terrorism
therm	heat	thermal, thermometer, thermos

Table 1.6. Common Root Words		
Root	**Meaning**	**Examples**
thesis	position	synthesis, hypothesis
venire, veni, ven	come, move toward	convention, contravene, intervene
vid, vis	to see	video, envision, evident, vision
voc	to call	voice, vocalize, advocate
zelos	ardor	zeal, zealous, zealot

Prefixes

A **prefix** is a set of letters that is added to the beginning of a word. Adding a prefix to a word can change its meaning. For instance, if you take the root word *jud*, which means *judge*, and add the prefix *pre–*, which means *before*, you create the word *prejudice*, which means to prejudge.

While prefixes cannot stand on their own as words, they do hold meaning. Learning to recognize common prefixes builds vocabulary and helps readers make educated guesses about unfamiliar words. It can also help improve reading comprehension in general. Table 1.7. lists some common prefixes, their meanings, and examples.

Table 1.7. Common Prefixes		
Prefix	**Meaning**	**Examples**
ambi–, amb–	around, on both sides	ambiguous, ambivalent
anti–	against, opposite	anticlimactic, antiseptic
bi–	two	bicycle, bifocals, bilingual
circum–, circa–	around, about	circumference, circadian, circumvent
com–, con–	with	communicate, convince
contra–	against	contradict, contrary, contravene
de–	reduce, remove	devalue, decelerate, decompose
di, dis–	not, opposite of	discontinue, disappear, discover, digress
en–, em–	cause to, into	enact, empower, embrace, enclose
fore–	before, front of	foreshadow, forebear

Table 1.7. Common Prefixes		
Prefix	**Meaning**	**Examples**
il–, im–, in–, ir–	not, without	illegal, impossible, invalidate, irresponsible
im–, in–	in, into	import, income
inter–	between, among	interrupt, intercept, intercede
mid–	middle	midterm, midway
mis–	bad, wrong	misinterpret, misspell
non–	not, without	nonconformist, nonfiction, nonviolent
over–	excessive	overeat, overconfident
peri–	around, about	perimeter, periphery
pre–	before	preexisting, precedent, preview
re–, red–	again, back, against, behind	recede, redo, retreat, rewrite
semi–	half, partial	semiconscious, semicircle
sub–	under	subway, submarine
super–	above, beyond	superfluous, superhuman, superior
trans–	across, over, through, beyond	transmit, transgression, transit
un–	not, opposite of	unusual, unashamed, unfair

Suffixes

A **suffix** is the same as a prefix except that a suffix is added to the end of a word rather than the beginning of a word. Table 1.8. lists some common prefixes, their meanings, and examples.

Table 1.8. Common Suffixes		
Suffix	**Meaning**	**Examples**
–able, –ible	is, can be	excitable, moveable, collectible
–al, –ial	having characteristics of, pertaining to	facial, procedural, universal
–cide, –cidum	kill	homicide, insecticide

Table 1.8. Common Suffixes		
Suffix	**Meaning**	**Examples**
–ed	past tense	arrested, called, treated
–en	made of, to cause to be	awaken, frighten, weaken
–er, –or	a person who	pioneer, professor, volunteer
–er	more	taller, meaner, shorter
–est	the most	fastest, meanest, shortest
–ful	full of	helpful, shameful, thankful
-ic	relating to, having characteristics of	poetic, dogmatic, organic
-ing	present participles, materials	sleeping, eating, bedding, frosting
–ion, –tion, –ation, –sion	act, process	submission, celebration, navigation
–ity, –cy –ty	state of, condition	activity, civility, normalcy, society
–ive, –ative, –itive	quality of	active, qualitative, sensitive
–ize	to make (forms verb)	compartmentalize, mechanize
–less	without	blameless, homeless, remorseless
–ly	in the manner of	bravely, courageously, horrifically
–ment	state of being, act of	contentment, placement, resentment
–ness	state of, condition of	weakness, kindness
–ology	study	biology, physiology, sociology
–ous, –eous, –ious	having qualities of, full of	riotous, hazardous, righteous, gracious
-y	characterized by	sassy, cheeky, slimy

The use of **context clues** is another strategy to determine the meaning of a word in a sentence. Context clues can appear in the same sentence as the unknown word or in sentences nearby. Context clues are discussed in more detail in the "Reading Comprehension" section.

Practice Questions

In the following questions, choose the word from the answer options that is closest in meaning to the underlined word.

16. The suspect did not have any <u>outstanding</u> warrants.
    (A) inactive
    (B) unsettled
    (C) unconfirmed
    (D) confirmed

17. Because a career in law enforcement can be dangerous, officers should not become <u>complacent</u>.
    (A) confident
    (B) unsafe
    (C) self-satisfied
    (D) cheerful

18. During her testimony, the witness <u>recanted</u> her statement.
    (A) affirmed
    (B) rescinded
    (C) retold
    (D) regretted

19. The jury did not believe that the suspect's mother was a <u>credible</u> witness.
    (A) trustworthy
    (B) likeable
    (C) suitable
    (D) useful

20. The suspect's account of the incident was full of <u>discrepancies</u>.
    (A) falsities
    (B) inaccuracies
    (C) deception
    (D) inconsistencies

Spelling

Why is spelling important in law enforcement? Much of what officers write is by hand, at least initially. What's more, any notes or other material an officer writes in connection with a crime or criminal investigation is **discoverable**. This means that the court can compel an officer to turn over his or her notes and communications to the court and lawyers for both sides. Right or wrong, spelling could affect the officer's credibility and competence in the eyes of a jury. Many people believe multiple spelling and grammatical errors show a lack of attention to detail and a tendency toward sloppy work, both of which are detrimental to effective police work.

Thankfully, there are numerous strategies to help you prepare for this portion of the exam. And, while you could simply relegate yourself to repetitively writing random words on a piece of paper, there are more focused methods to improve your performance on a multiple-choice spelling test. Learning the following tips, tricks, and rules can help you prevent common spelling errors.

Homophones

Homophones are words that sound alike but are spelled differently and hold different meanings, such as *break* and *brake*.

Officer Brady stepped on the brake to stop the car.

Officer Brady took a lunch break during his shift.

Commonly Confused Words

- **ACCEPT:** agree
- **EXCEPT:** not including
- **ALOUD:** said out loud
- **ALLOWED:** able to
- **BARE:** uncovered
- **BEAR:** large animal; to carry
- **BRAKE:** to stop
- **BREAK:** to damage or interrupt
- **DIE:** to no longer be alive
- **DYE:** to artificially change color
- **EFFECT:** result (noun)
- **AFFECT:** to change (verb)
- **FLOUR:** used for cooking
- **FLOWER:** grows out of the ground
- **HEAL:** to get better
- **HEEL:** the back part of the foot
- **HOLE:** an opening
- **WHOLE:** all of something
- **INSURE:** to have insurance (*I need to insure my car.*)
- **ENSURE:** to make sure something happens (*She ensured that the dog found a good home.*)
- **MEAT:** the flesh of an animal
- **MEET:** to see someone
- **MORNING:** the start of the day
- **MOURNING:** grieving
- **PATIENCE:** tolerating annoyances
- **PATIENTS:** people receiving medical care
- **PEACE:** not at war
- **PIECE:** a part of something
- **POOR:** having very little money
- **POUR:** to dispense from a container
- **PRINCIPAL:** the leader or administrative head of a school
- **PRINCIPLE:** a strongly held belief
- **RAIN:** precipitation
- **REIN:** a strap that controls an animal
- **REIGN:** to rule over

- **RIGHT:** correct; a legal entitlement
- **RITE:** a ritual
- **WRITE:** to put words on paper
- **STAIR:** used to get from one floor to another
- **STARE:** a long, fixed look
- **SUITE:** a set of rooms
- **SWEET:** the taste associated with sugar
- **THEIR:** belonging to them (*they brought their luggage*)
- **THERE:** a place (*the luggage is over there*)
- **THEY'RE:** they are (*they're looking for the luggage*)
- **THROUGH:** to go in one side and out the other
- **THREW:** tossed (past tense of *throw*)
- **TO:** the preposition indicating movement or purpose (*I am going to work to do my job*)
- **TOO:** in addition (*I'm coming too*)
- **TWO:** more than one; dual (*two officers patrol this area together*)
- **WEAR:** to put on (*I'll wear my new dress.*)
- **WHERE:** to question about place (*Where is the door?*)
- **YOUR:** belonging to you (*your car*)
- **YOU'RE:** you are (*you're going to need a new car*

Some words are similar in meaning but are not actually synonyms. Such words are commonly confused in both writing and speech, and a hallmark of good writing is being able to use these words properly. Some of the most commonly confused words are listed in Table 1.9.

Table 1.9. Commonly Confused Words	
WORDS	**DEFINITION**
Amount	describes a noncountable quantity (*an unknown amount of jewelry was stolen*)
Number	describes a countable quantity (*an unknown number of necklaces was stolen*)
Bring	toward the speaker (*bring to me*)
Take	away from the speaker (*take away from me*)
Farther	a measurable distance (*the house farther up the road*)
Further	more or greater (*explain further what you mean*)
Fewer	a smaller amount of something plural and countable (*fewer chairs*)

Table 1.9. Commonly Confused Words	
WORDS	**DEFINITION**
Less	a smaller amount of something that cannot be counted (*less water*)
Lose	to fail to win; to not be able to find something (*to lose a game; to lose one's keys*)
Loose	relaxed; not firmly in place (*my pants are loose*)

Special Spelling Rules

Generally, the letter *i* comes before the letter *e* in a word except when the *i* is preceded by the letter *c*:

- *piece*
- *salient*
- *ceiling*
- *conceivable*

There are some notable exceptions where the letter *e* comes before the letter *i*:

- words that end in–*cie*, like *proficient* or *ancient*
- plural words ending in –*cies*, like *policies*
- words with an *ay* sound, like *eight*, *vein*, or *neighbor*

Helpful Hint:

The "*i* comes before *e* except after *c*": rule has many exceptions: "Your foreign neighbors weighed the iciest beige glaciers!"

When adding a suffix to a word, change the final *y* to an *i*:

lazy → *laziest*

tidy → *tidily*

For words that end with the letters –*le*, replace the letter *e* with the letter *y*:

subtle → *subtly*

Plurals

Regular nouns are made plural by adding the letter *s*. Irregular nouns can follow many different rules for pluralization. These rules are summarized in Table 1.10.

Table 1.10. Irregular Plural Nouns		
Ends With:	**Make It Plural By:**	**Example**
y	changing *y* to *i* and adding –*es*	baby → babies
f	changing *f* to *v* and adding –*es*	leaf → leaves

Table 1.10. Irregular Plural Nouns		
Ends With:	**Make It Plural By:**	**Example**
fe	changing *f* to *v* and adding *–s*	knife → knives
o	adding *–es*	potato → potatoes
us	changing *–us* to *–i*	nucleus → nuclei

Always the Same	**Doesn't Follow the Rules**
sheep	man → men
deer	child → children
fish	person → people
pants	goose → geese
binoculars	mouse → mice
scissors	ox → oxen

Pluralize words ending in *–ch, –s, –sh, –x,* or *–z* by adding *–es* to the end:

catch → catches

pass → passes

push → pushes

annex → annexes

blitz → blitzes

An exception to the *–ch* rule includes words where the *ch* makes a *k* sound. For those words, simply add the letter *s* to the end of the word:

stomach → stomachs

Possessives Versus Contractions

A **CONTRACTION** is a combination of two words that is shortened by using an apostrophe to indicate the missing letter or letters. For instance, *cannot* is shortened to *can't*; the apostrophe stands in for the missing letters *n* and *o*.

A **POSSESSIVE** is a word with an apostrophe added to indicate possession. For example, rather than writing "the duty belt that belongs to Pat," write "Pat's duty belt."

The suspect's car was badly damaged.

A notable exception to this rule—and a common mistake—is the improper use of the contraction *it's* as the possessive, *its*. The contraction for *it is* or *it has* is *it's*:

It's dangerous in that area of town at night.

The word *its* is possessive and shows ownership of the pronoun *it*:

The jury reached its verdict.

Its license plate was obscured.

Conjugating Verbs

The suffixes *–ed* or *–ing* added to a regular verb generally signify the verb's tense. For example, the present tense of the verb *to question* is *question*:

You question the suspect while I write the report.

To show that the event happened in the past (or to form the past tense), the word *question* becomes *questioned*. And to refer to an action that is still happening (or to form the present participle), *question* becomes *questioning*. (See "Common Grammatical Errors" above for more details on conjugating verbs.)

There are some exceptions to the general rules for conjugating regular verbs. For verbs ending with a silent *–e*, drop the *–e* before adding *–ed* or *–ing*:

fake → faked → faking

ache → ached → aching

When verbs end in the letters *–ee,* do not drop the second *e*; instead, simply add *–d* or *–ing*:

free → freed → freeing

agree → agreed → agreeing

When the verb ends with a single vowel plus a consonant, and the stress is at the end of the word, then the consonant must be doubled before adding *–ed* or *–ing*:

commit → committed → committing

refer → referred → referring

If the stress is not at the end of the word, then the consonant can remain singular:

target → targeted → targeting

visit → visited → visiting

Verbs that end with the letter *c* must have the letter *k* added before receiving a suffix:

panic → panicked → panicking

Practice Questions

Read the following sentences and choose the correct spelling of the missing word.

21. The defendant asked the court to show him ______ in the punishment for his crime.
    (A) lienency
    (B) leniency
    (C) leneincy
    (D) leanency

22. Deputy Smith found ____________ in the inmate's cell.
   (A) contriband
   (B) controband
   (C) contraband
   (D) contraband

23. Evidence that is fleeting or that can fade away over time is said to be of an ________ nature.
   (A) effervescent
   (B) evanecent
   (C) evanescent
   (D) evenescent

24. Officer Jones attempted to _______ the victim's blood loss by applying pressure to the wound.
   (A) mitagate
   (B) mitegate
   (C) midigate
   (D) mitigate

Answer Key

1. C: *Minnesota* and *August* are proper nouns, and *coat* and *gloves* are common nouns. *I* is a pronoun, and *warm* is an adjective that modifies *coat*.

2. A: *New* modifies the noun *chef*, and *boiling* modifies the noun *soup*.

3. C: The correct preposition is *of*. The preposition *of* usually shows a relationship and may accompany a verb.

4. A: Option A should use quotation marks to set off a direct quote: *"I love apple pie!" John exclaimed with a smile.*

5. B: The sentence is a question, so it should end with a question mark.

6. A: The phrase is a prepositional phrase beginning with the preposition *with*. The preposition *with* modifies *the eager students*.

7. A: In this sentence, the conjunction is joining together two contrasting ideas, so the correct answer is *but*.

8. B: *The members of the band* is plural (*members*), so it should be replaced by the plural pronoun *their* instead of the singular *her*.

9. B: Option A contains a vague reference; it is unclear who was shot.

10. B: This sentence contains a verb error; the verb *is* should be plural: *are*. All plural indefinite pronouns agree with plural verbs. Here, the subject of the sentence, *some*, is a plural indefinite pronoun, so it requires a plural verb.

11. A: The phrase *by this time tomorrow* describes an action that will take place and be completed in the future, so the future perfect tense (*will have arrived*) should be used.

12. D: This sentence should read, "Of the four speeches, Jerry's was the longest." The word *long* has only one syllable, so it should be modified with the suffix *–est*, not the word *most*.

13. A: Option B has a misplaced modifier (the word *often*).

14. A: Option B contains a sentence fragment.

15. B: Option A is a run-on sentence.

16. B: *Unsettled* means *outstand- ing* or *due*.

17. C: *Self-satisfied* means *complacent*.

18. B: *Rescinded* means *recanted*.

19. A: *Trustworthy* means *credible*.

20. D: *Inconsistencies* means *discrepancies*.

21. B: *Leniency* is the correct spelling.

22. C: *Contraband* is the correct spelling.

23. C: *Evanescent* is the correct spelling.

24. D: *Mitigate* is the correct spelling.

Reading Comprehension

In the land of movies and television, law enforcement officers are rarely shown reading. Dirty Harry, John McClane, Horatio Caine, or Andy Sipowicz would be hard-pressed to pick up the penal code, case notes, or even a newspaper! But in the real world, reading is a huge part of a law enforcement officer's job.

> **Did You Know?**
>
> You do not need to use outside knowledge on reading comprehension questions. Remember, the answer is located within the passage.

Law enforcement officers spend a considerable amount of time reading reports, case law, statutes, subpoenas, warrants, investigative notes, memos and policy changes, news reports about policing and the community, and more. Understanding what you read is paramount because it may dictate how you do the job, and misunderstanding what you read could cost you your job.

Reading comprehension is one of the most important aspects of law enforcement. The PELLETB tests applicants' reading comprehension abilities by presenting a passage to read and then asking several questions about the passage's content. The following information provides tips and tricks to improve your skills and navigate the reading comprehension section of the exam.

Reading for Understanding

Reading for understanding is different from reading for entertainment. Rather than simply skimming a passage for generalized information, the reader must dig more deeply into the text, make inferences and connections, and evaluate and interpret ideas and information. An integral part of reading comprehension, however, is being able to answer questions about the information. To be proficient at comprehension, readers must master several tasks while reading a particular passage:

> **Helpful Hint:**
>
> During conversations, law enforcement officers often summarize. To ensure understanding, officers may use their own words to repeat information a victim or suspect provides. The victim or suspect generally confirms or adjusts the restated information. To practice summarizing, take the most important information from something you have just read and restate it in your own words.

Differentiate fact from opinion. Many readers cannot tell the differences between fact and opinion. Contrary to popular belief, fact and opinion are not opposites; instead, they are differing types of statements:

- A **fact** is a statement that can be proven by direct or objective evidence. Juries are called the "finders of fact" because they use the evidence presented to prove a statement.
- An **opinion**, though it may be based in fact, is a statement established using belief or judgment and cannot be objectively proven to be true or false. Opinions are not necessarily wrong; they simply are not facts.

Distinguish between what is important and what is simply interesting. When determining what is important in a passage, think about the main point and tone:

- What is the author trying to say?
- What is the main point?

Information that tends to strengthen or weaken the main point is *important*. Information that does not strengthen or weaken the main point is simply *interesting*.

Determine cause-and-effect relationships. Determine if there is a cause-and-effect relationship between pieces of information contained in the passage. Determining cause-and-effect relationships is important in comprehension as well as in establishing potential outcomes. Look for words that show causal relationships:

- *because*
- *since*
- *therefore*
- *thus*
- *so*

Helpful Hint:

Read the passage carefully. **Do not skim the passage.** Read it two or three times to ensure you understand what the passage is communicating. Remember: This section is examining *comprehension*. Reading too quickly can cause you to miss important information.

Compare and contrast ideas and information. Connecting words often indicate transition within a passage. Understanding transitions can help keep you on track with the author's main point, rather than confusing you with opposing points of view in the passage. Look for words that show a shift in the author's position:

- *however*
- *but*
- *rather*
- *in contrast*
- *although*

Draw conclusions. Law enforcement officers regularly make inferences, draw conclusions, and make determinations based on information presented. After reading the passage, ask yourself the following:

- What judgments can be made based on the information provided?
- What evidence included in the passage supports that judgment?
- Are there other interpretations that can be made using the provided information and evidence?

Question Types

Reading comprehension tests generally use seven basic question types, which are explored in more detail in this chapter:

- **What is the main point?** These questions ask you to identify the author's thesis or hypothesis. A question stem relating to this question type might ask, "The passage was primarily concerned with which of the following?" Check the thesis statement or conclusion for the answer to these types of questions.
- **What is the supporting idea?** These questions generally ask you to locate specific information. A question stem relating to this question type might ask, "The passage mentions each of the following EXCEPT..." You may need to reread the passage to find the correct answer. You might look for keywords in the answer options to help steer you in the right direction.
- **Drawing inferences.** Questions that require you to draw inferences often ask, "The passage implies which of the following?" The answer options will generally closely imitate the text of the passage and rely upon specific facts provided.
- **What is the tone?** These questions ask you to identify the author's attitude. Question stems generally ask, "The author's tone is best described as..."
- **Apply the theme to other circumstances.** Questions requiring you to apply information from the passage to a similar situation often take the following form: "The author would most likely agree with which of the following?" There are no shortcuts or tricks to answering these question types. The best strategy is to be able to identify the heart of the passage and relate it to similar answer options.
- **Logical reasoning.** This question style is the reverse of the "Application" question style. Logical reasoning questions ask you to take information from *outside* the passage and apply it to the passage to make determinations. An example of a logical reasoning question might be "Which of the following, if true, would most weaken the main point of the second paragraph?" Understanding the author's main point or argument and using your reasoning abilities to determine the value of answer options will help you answer these questions.
- **Relating different ideas.** These questions require you to determine the relationship between different ideas or parts of the passage. Questions are framed in a variety of ways, but they might ask how two paragraphs relate to each other or how an idea in one sentence contrasts with an idea later in the passage.

Helpful Hint:

Read the passage *before* you read the question. Reading the question first can distract you from the main point of the passage. Errors are more likely to happen if you answer the question prematurely and without full understanding of it.

Topic and Main Idea

The **topic** is a word or short phrase that explains what a passage is about. The **main idea** is a complete sentence that explains what the author is trying to say about the topic.

Generally, the **topic sentence** is the first (or near the first) sentence in a paragraph. It is a general statement that introduces the topic so that the reader knows what to expect.

> **Helpful Hint:**
>
> To find the main idea, identify the topic and then ask yourself, "What is the author trying to tell me about the topic?"

The **summary sentence**, on the other hand, frequently (but not always!) comes at the end of a paragraph or passage because it wraps up all of the ideas presented. This sentence summarizes what an author has said about the topic. Some passages, particularly short ones, will not include a summary sentence.

Table 2.1. Identifying Topic and Main Idea	
Noise complaints are one of the most common calls received by police officers in cities and suburban areas. Close quarters and strong personalities make it more likely that neighbors will butt heads; the job of officers is to keep the peace. Usually, an officer can solve the problem by warning the offender. Most people will immediately turn down their music or end a late-night party when they find out they risk a hefty fine. On rare occasions, officers will issue citations for violating city ordinances or will arrest offenders for crimes like disorderly conduct.	
Topic	Noise complaints are one of the most common calls received by police officers in cities and suburban areas.
Summary	Close quarters and strong personalities make it more likely that neighbors will butt heads; the job of officers is to keep the peace.
Main	To restore order, officers respond to noise complaints, which are very common in crowded areas.

Practice Questions

1. Topic

Police dogs usually work from six to nine years. K-9 officers have a variety of professional responsibilities: sniffing out explosives and narcotics, finding missing persons and human remains, and protecting officers. Many K-9 officers retire to live a comfortable life with their handlers, who know them better than anyone.

What is the topic of the passage?

(A) dog lifespan
(B) police dogs
(C) dog handlers
(D) canine retirement

2. Main Idea

The Battle of the Little Bighorn, commonly called Custer's Last Stand, was a battle between the Seventh Cavalry Regiment of the US Army and the combined forces of the Lakota, the Northern Cheyenne, and the Arapaho tribes. Led by war leaders Crazy Horse and Chief Gall, and religious leader Sitting Bull, the allied tribes of the Plains Indians decisively defeated their US foes. Two hundred and sixty-eight US soldiers were killed, including Lieutenant Colonel George Armstrong Custer, two of his brothers, his nephew, his brother-in-law, and six Indian scouts.

What is the main idea of this passage?

(A) Most of Custer's family died in the Battle of the Little Bighorn.
(B) The Seventh Cavalry Regiment was formed to fight Native American tribes.
(C) Sitting Bull and George Custer were fierce enemies.
(D) The Battle of the Little Bighorn was a significant victory for the Plains Indians.

Supporting Details

Statements that describe or explain the main idea are **supporting details**. Supporting details are often found after the topic sentence. They support the main idea through examples, descriptions, and explanations.

Authors may add details to support their arguments or claims. As discussed earlier, **facts**, are details that point to truths, while **opinions** are based on personal beliefs or judgments. To differentiate between facts and opinions, look for statements that express feelings, attitudes, or beliefs that cannot be proven (opinions) and statements that can be proven (facts).

Helpful Hint:

To find supporting details, look for sentences that connect to the main idea and tell more about it.

Table 2.2. Supporting Details and Fact and Opinion	
Police academies have strict physical requirements for cadets. Cadets must pass fitness tests and train daily. As a result, some new recruits worry about their physical fitness before heading into the academy. Some graduates suggest focusing on core strength. Others believe that boxing is the best workout. We feel that cardiovascular activity is the most important exercise.	
SUPPORTING DETAILS	Cadets must pass fitness tests and train daily.
FACT	Police academies have strict physical requirements for cadets.
OPINION	We feel that cardiovascular activity is the most important exercise.

Practice Questions

3. Supporting Details

Increasingly, companies are turning to subcontracting services rather than hiring full-time employees. This provides companies with advantages like greater flexibility, reduced legal responsibility to employees, and a lower possibility of unionization within the company; however, this has also led to increasing confusion and uncertainty over the legal definition of employment. Courts have grappled with questions about the hiring company's responsibility in maintaining fair labor practices. Companies argue that they delegate that authority to subcontractors, while unions and other worker advocate groups argue that companies still have a legal obligation to the workers who contribute to their businesses.

Which detail BEST supports the idea that contracting employees is beneficial to companies?

(A) Uncertainty over the legal definition of employment increases.
(B) Companies still have a legal obligation to contractors.
(C) There is a lower possibility of unionization within the company.
(D) Contractors, not companies, control fair labor practices.

4. Fact and Opinion

An officer cited a motorist for reckless driving. The driver was performing unsafe maneuvers. The motorist was "doing donuts," rotating the vehicle. The officer observed this activity in a parking lot after dark. The officer wrote a citation. In addition, the vehicle was impounded.

Which statement from the passage is an opinion?

(A) An officer cited a motorist for reckless driving.
(B) The driver was performing unsafe maneuvers.
(C) The motorist was "doing donuts," rotating the vehicle.
(D) In addition, the vehicle was impounded.

Drawing Conclusions

Helpful Hint:

When drawing conclusions, look for facts, character actions and dialogue, how each sentence connects to the topic, and the author's reasoning for an argument.

Readers can use information that is **explicit**, or clearly stated, along with information that is **implicit**, or indirect, to make inferences and **draw conclusions**. Readers can determine meaning from what is implied by using details, context clues, and prior knowledge. When answering questions, consider what is known from personal experiences and make note of all of the information the author has provided before drawing a conclusion.

Table 2.3. Drawing Conclusions	
When the Spanish-American War broke out in 1898, the US Army was small and understaffed. President William McKinley called for 1,250 volunteers to serve in the First US Volunteer Cavalry. The ranks were quickly filled by cowboys, gold prospectors, hunters, gamblers, Native Americans, veterans, police officers, and college students looking for an adventure. The officer corps was composed of veterans of previous wars. With more volunteers than it could accept, the army set high standards: all of the recruits had to be skilled on horseback and with guns. Consequently, they became known as the Rough Riders.	
Question	Why are the volunteers named Rough Riders?
Explicit Information	Different people volunteered, men were looking for adventure, recruits had to be extremely skilled on horseback and with guns due to a glut of volunteers.
Implicit Information	Men had previous occupations; officer corps veterans worked with volunteers.
Conclusion Drawn	The men were called Rough Riders because they were inexperienced yet enthusiastic to help with the war and were willing to put in extra effort to join.

Practice Question

5. Drawing Conclusions

"Swatting" is a dangerous practice. Someone falsely reports a crime in progress at a location to attract a large number of police to the site. The false crime usually involves hostages or a similar violent scenario, so police are prepared for confrontation. In fact, the term swatting *is derived from the name for those police who specialize in such situations—the SWAT team, which carries high-caliber weapons and deploys flash bangs and tear gas. In a swatting incident, innocent citizens are shocked by a sudden police raid on their home; likewise, police ready to face a violent perpetrator are surprised to find a family eating dinner or watching TV. The confusion caused by the false information and urgency of the raid make it very dangerous for all involved. Tragic outcomes are not uncommon.*

Which conclusion about the effects of swatting is most likely true?

(A) Swatting is increasingly common, thanks to social media.
(B) Swatting mostly occurs where there are large SWAT teams.
(C) Swatting is usually harmless, though a waste of police time.
(D) Swatting can result in injury or death to innocent citizens or officers.

The Author's Purpose and Point of View

The **author's purpose** describes the author's reason for writing a text. Authors may write for several reasons:

- to share an experience
- to entertain
- to persuade
- to inform readers

Authors can achieve their purpose by using the following types of writing:

- persuasive
- expository
- narrative

> **Helpful Hint:**
>
> Use the acronym **P.I.E.S.**—*persuade, inform, entertain, state*—to help you remember elements of an author's purpose.

Persuasive writing influences the actions and thoughts of readers. Authors state an opinion and then provide reasons that support that opinion. **Expository writing** outlines and explains steps in a process; authors focus on a sequence of events. **Narrative writing** tells a story. Authors include a setting, plot, characters, problem, and solution in the text.

Authors also share their **points of view** (perspectives, attitudes, and beliefs) with readers. Identify an author's point of view by word choice, details, descriptions, and characters' actions. The author's attitude, or **tone**, can be found in word choices that conveys feelings or stances on a topic.

Text structure is the way in which the author organizes a text. A text can be organized to show problem and solution, comparison and contrast, or even cause and effect. The structure of a text can give insight into an author's purpose and point of view. If a text is organized to pose an argument or advertise a product, it can be considered persuasive. The author's point of view will be revealed in how thoughts and opinions are expressed in the text.

Table 2.4. The Author's Purpose and Point of View	
Officer ride-alongs are great ways for community members to get to know law enforcement officers. They offer a valuable opportunity for students, journalists, community leaders, and those considering a career in law enforcement to learn more about the day-to-day experiences of police business. In a ride-along, you join an officer as he or she responds to calls, stops cars, and interacts with the public. Riders can ask questions and see the world from the perspective of a cop. Ride-alongs are wonderful ways for members of the public to learn about policing.	
Author's Purpose	persuade readers of the benefit of ride-alongs
Point of View	advocates ride-alongs as "great ways for community members to get to know law enforcement officers"

Tone	positive, encouraging, pointing out the benefits of ride-alongs, using positive words like *great* and *wonderful*
Structure	descriptive: describes ride-alongs, giving specific examples to support the argument that they are valuable

Practice Questions

6. Author's Purpose

Several law enforcement departments in the United States have implemented sUAS (small unmanned aircraft systems), or drone programs. Drones provide intelligence, surveillance, and reconnaissance, known as ISR, helping inform decision-makers in reconstructing accidents and crime scenes, finding victims in search and rescue, and managing fire scenes. Local jurisdictions, such as the Los Angeles County Sheriff's Department, use drones as do federal agencies like the US Border Patrol. What was once a military tool is becoming a valuable resource for law enforcement.

What is the purpose of this passage?

(A) to argue that drones are important for patrol
(B) to explain the history of drones in law enforcement
(C) to persuade readers that drone programs should be funded
(D) to describe how drones are used by law enforcement agencies

7. Point of View

Any law enforcement officer should expect to use force on the job at some point. Fortunately, officers have many nonlethal options for controlling a suspect or situation. Tasers, pepper spray, and batons are all effective for neutralizing a threat in many circumstances. Officers also train in basic ground and hand-to-hand tactics; however, if possible, they should avoid physical encounters for safety reasons. In certain situations, though, officers must use their service pistols, which may result in fatalities.

Which of the following BEST describes what the author believes?

(A) Most forms of nonlethal force are effective, but not all.
(B) Lethal force should never be used because it is unethical.
(C) Officers should use nonlethal force if possible.
(D) Physical encounters should always be avoided.

8. Tone

Managing people is complicated in any field, and law enforcement is no different. Managers must balance administrative, financial, disciplinary, and policy responsibilities. Good managers also need to be aware of their subordinates' mental health in stressful fields like law enforcement.

Recognizing the signs of stress, depression, substance abuse, and afflictions like post-traumatic stress disorder (PTSD) is an important skill for those who manage law enforcement personnel. The department can provide officers with support for mental wellness, improving their job performance and safety. The sooner a supervisor can spot symptoms, the faster the officer can receive assistance.

Which of the following best describes the author's attitude toward officers' mental health?

(A) dismissive
(B) sympathetic
(C) pitying
(D) angry

9. Text Structure

Increasingly, police departments require law enforcement officers to wear body cameras when they interact with members of the public. Some officers agree with this policy because the cameras provide protection against false complaints of police misconduct. Footage can exonerate police officers, proving their professionalism in situations. Other officers are cautious, worried that the cameras could limit officer discretion. Their concern is that supervisors might review and second-guess the officers' decisions during a call. What is undeniable is that the trend of body cameras is not going away as more jurisdictions across America adopt them.

What is the structure of this text?

(A) cause and effect
(B) order and sequence
(C) problem and solution
(D) compare and contrast

Comparing Passages

Sometimes readers need to compare and contrast two texts. After reading and identifying the main idea of each text, look for similarities and differences in the main idea, details, claims, evidence, characters, and so on.

When answering questions about two texts, first identify whether the question is about a similarity or a difference, and then look for specific details in the text that connect to the answers. After that, determine which answer option best describes the similarity or difference.

Helpful Hint:

Use a Venn diagram, table, or highlighters to organize similarities and differences between texts.

Table 2.5. Comparing Passages	
Intranasally Administered Naloxone *Because even tiny amounts of the dangerous narcotic fentanyl can result in overdose or death, many law enforcement officers carry the anti-overdose drug naloxone in case they encounter the frequently abused substance. Naloxone can be administered intranasally, allowing for rapid absorption into the bloodstream. The rescuer lays the victim on his or her back and sprays the medication into one nostril. The rescuer needs minimal training to administer naloxone in this way.* **Injectable Naloxone** *Naloxone, a medication that counteracts opioid overdose, is carried by many law enforcement officers in case of accidental contact with powerful narcotics like fentanyl. Naloxone must be injected by trained first responders. Injectable naloxone is effective when the nasal cavity is damaged if, for instance, the victim has head trauma. Injectable naloxone is also used on detection dogs that have accidentally inhaled fentanyl or another opioid and need a lower dose of naloxone than a human would.*	
Similarities	Both substances are used by law enforcement to fight accidental opioid overdoses.
Differences (Contrast)	Intranasally administered naloxone works rapidly and can be given by anyone. Injectable naloxone must be administered by a trained first responder and is more effective in specific situations.

Practice Question

10. Comparing Passages

Self-Driving Cars: A Safer America

Self-driving cars, already present on our streets, are the wave of the future. They will make roads safer. Unlike human drivers, self-driving cars don't drink and drive, get lost in conversation, or fumble with phones. They can also be programmed to strictly adhere to the speed limit and traffic laws. That makes them the best bet for road and highway safety. Law enforcement officials will have more time to pursue violent criminals if they don't need to spend as much time monitoring highways for speeders and unsafe drivers.

The Dangers of Autonomous Vehicles

Many people are excited about autonomous vehicles, or self-driving cars, but they are risky machines. Already, several have been involved in deadly accidents, failing to brake for pedestrians or making inappropriate turns resulting in wrecks. Autonomous vehicles can malfunction; they occupy a gray area for law enforcement: What if an autonomous vehicle is speeding? How can highway patrol pull it over? What is the role of the traffic officer in an accident caused by a self-driving car? Who is accountable? There is no substitution for an experienced human driver with good judgment.

Which of these statements BEST compares the information in both texts?

(A) Autonomous vehicles are a social advantage.
(B) People are already using self-driving cars.
(C) Self-driving cars occupy a legal gray area.
(D) Officers will benefit from self-driving cars.

Transition Words

Transition words and phrases connect different ideas within sentences or between paragraphs in a text. Because they lend order and structure to sentences and paragraphs, transition words aid in reading comprehension.

There are many different kinds of transition words. For example, passages may include transition words that suggest **similarities**:

- *and*
- *in addition*
- *similarly*
- *also*

She received a ticket for her expired registration; she ***also*** *got a ticket for not having a license.*

In the example above, the word *also* connects the first clause with the second clause. The woman was ticketed for her expired registration, and she *also* received an additional ticket for not having a license.

Transition words can also suggest **opposites**. Look for words like *however*, *on the other hand*, *but*, *although*, and *conversely*.

There seemed to be ample evidence in favor of the defendant;
however, he was found guilty at trial.

In the example, the word *however* signals to the reader that the following clause will have an opposite meaning to the idea that precedes it. With a lot of evidence in favor of the defendant, chances are he would be found not guilty, but the word *however* indicates that the opposite of what was expected took place: that the defendant was found guilty.

Meanings of Words

To understand the meanings of unfamiliar words, use **context clues**. Context clues are hints that the author provides to help readers define difficult words. They can be found in words or phrases in the same sentence or in neighboring sentences. Look for synonyms, antonyms, definitions, examples, and explanations in the text to determine the meaning of the unfamiliar word.

Sometimes parts of a word can make its meaning easier to determine. **Affixes** are added to **root words** (a word's basic form) to modify meaning; they include prefixes and suffixes, as discussed earlier in the "Vocabulary" section:

- **Prefixes** are added to the beginning of root words.
- **Suffixes** are added to the ends of root words.

It is helpful to deconstruct words into parts, finding meaning in each part. Take, for example, the word *unjustifiable* : the prefix is *un–* (*not*), the root word is *justify* ("to prove reasonable"), and the suffix is –*able* (referring to a quality).

Another way to determine the meaning of unknown words is to consider their denotations and connotations with other words in the sentence:

- **Denotation** is the literal meaning of a word.
- **Connotation** is the positive or negative associations of a word.

> **Helpful Hint:**
>
> Use what you know about a word to figure out its meaning, and then look for clues in the sentence or paragraph.

Authors use words to convey thoughts. When the meanings of the words in context differ from the literal meanings of the words, it is known as **figurative language**. Types of figurative language include similes, metaphors, hyperboles, and personification:

- **Similes** compare two things that are not alike; they use the words *like* or *as*.
- **Metaphors** are used to compare two things that are not exactly alike but may share a certain characteristic.
- **Hyperboles** are statements that exaggerate something to make a point or to draw attention to a certain feature.
- **Personification** involves using human characteristics to describe an animal or object.

Table 2.6. Meanings of Words	
Check fraud used to be a major crime, but today fewer people than ever use paper checks. Still, criminals continue to find ways to steal from consumers. Identity theft is a threat to all Americans as more people use credit cards and electronic financial applications than cash. Despite encryption techniques that protect personal details, computer hackers periodically uncover consumers' financial information in security breaches. Small-time thieves steal credit cards, use card skimmers at gas stations, or make fake cards with specialized machines.	
Context Clues	Techniques *protect* personal details; the details are still *uncovered* for criminal use.

Affixes	The prefix *en–* in *encryption* means *cause to*. The suffix *–ion* suggests an act or process.
Roots	The root of the word *encryption* is *crypt*, which means *hide* or *conceal*.
Meaning	*Encryption* means "the process of causing something to be hidden."

Practice Questions

11. Context Clues

After a few high-profile missing-persons cases in the 1970s and 1980s, parents in many communities became concerned about "stranger danger." Families worried that their children would be abducted, taken by criminal outsiders.

However, when a child goes missing, the perpetrator is usually someone the child knows. Family members make up the majority of perpetrators in cases of missing children. It is very rare that a child is kidnapped by a total stranger, though it can happen.

What does the word *abducted* mean as it is used in the passage?

(A) taken by criminal outsiders
(B) the perpetrator
(C) family members make up
(D) "stranger danger"

12. Root Words and Affixes

Unfortunately, automobile accidents happen. The good news is, most result in only minor damage to vehicles. Still, drivers are responsible for calling the police and reporting the incident, regardless of its severity. An officer will arrive to take the statement of each driver and survey the scene. The officer will closely examine the drivers' behavior and mannerisms to determine if their claims are credible. After all the evidence is collected, reviewed, and approved, the insurance company assigns blame to one party. The officer's role is key in this determination.

Based on affixes and context clues, what does *credible* mean?

(A) believable
(B) achievable
(C) likeable
(D) noticeable

13. Figurative Language

Nothing in the world is harder than waking up for a job you don't love. Who wants to drag themselves to work every day? That's why it's important to follow your passions. Many say that serving the public in law enforcement is more than just a job; it's a calling. Police officers risk their lives to serve and protect the public. It takes a certain kind of person to thrive in law enforcement.

Which type of figurative language is used in the second sentence?

(A) simile
(B) metaphor
(C) personification
(D) hyperbole

Answer Key

1. B: The topic of the passage is police dogs. The passage mentions how long they work, their handlers, and the usual retirement circumstances of police dogs as supporting ideas.

2. D: The author writes that "the allied tribes . . . decisively defeated their US foes," and the remainder of the passage provides details to support this idea.

3. C: The passage specifically presents this detail as one of the advantages of subcontracting services.

4. B: The statement "The driver was performing unsafe maneuvers" is a judgment about the safety of the actions taken by the driver. The driver (or his attorney) might argue that his driving was safe.

5. D: The passage states that swatting is dangerous because of confusion caused by false information and the nature of a violent raid. The sentence "Tragic outcomes are not uncommon" suggests that injury or death can happen.

6. D: The text provides details on how drones are used and what departments use them.

7. C: The author discusses many options for nonlethal force, using the word *fortunately* to show a preference for it; however, the author also allows that lethal force is sometimes necessary.

8. B: The author states that "[t]he department can provide officers with support" and that supervisors should "be aware of their subordinates' mental health." By taking these positions, the author is being sympathetic and supportive of officers' mental health.

9. D: In this text, two perspectives on body cameras are compared and contrasted.

10. B: Both passages indicate that self-driving cars, or autonomous vehicles, are already in use.

11. A: The phrase "taken by criminal outsiders" redefines the word *abducted* in the sentence.

12. A: The root *cred* means *believe*. The words *evidence*, *reviewed*, and *approved* are context clues hinting that something needs to be believed and accepted.

13. B: The writer uses the metaphor *drag*. No one literally drags himself or herself to work.

Practice Test #1

Writing

Clarity

Directions: In the following sentence pairs, identify the sentence that is most clearly written.

1.
   A) Julie was happy to get back to her life after the trial she felt she received justice.
   B) Julie was happy to get back to her life after the trial. She felt she received justice.

2.
   A) Marge told Ruth that Marge's supervisor wanted to speak with Ruth.
   B) Marge told Ruth that her supervisor wanted to speak with her.

3.
   A) Kelly did not see the cyclist riding in her blind spot, and she hit him with her car as she made the right turn.
   B) Kelly did not see the cyclist riding in her blind spot, and she hit him with her car. As she made the right turn.

4.
   A) Officers who train rarely are caught off guard.
   B) Officers who train are rarely caught off guard.

5.
   A) The defendant was angry at the sentence he received. He antagonized the judge out of frustration.
   B) The defendant was angry at the sentence he received he antagonized the judge out of frustration.

6.
   A) Police officers who keep up to date with changing laws, policies, and community priorities tend to be more successful than those who do not, unless they are assigned to special covert details that have little contact with ordinary citizens.
   B) Police officers who keep up to date with changing laws, policies, and community priorities tend to be more successful. Than those who do not unless they are assigned to special covert details that have little contact with ordinary citizens.

7.
   A) Jake and Ronald were playing cards when Ronald shot Jake. In the leg.
   B) Jake and Ronald were playing cards when Ronald shot Jake in the leg.

8.

A) Community leaders and law enforcement officers often work together toward common goals. Proactive problem solving and preventing social discord are two such goals.

B) Community leaders and law enforcement officers often work together toward common goals proactive problem solving and preventing social discord are two such goals.

9.

A) Detective Sherman almost got convictions for every felony arrest he ever made.

B) Detective Sherman got convictions for almost every arrest he ever made.

10.

A) Family law courtrooms are among the most dangerous because emotions run high when dealing with family issues.

B) Family law courtrooms are among the most dangerous because emotions run high. When dealing with family issues.

11.

A) Kyle wanted to sing, dance, and act; it is what made him happy.

B) Kyle wanted to sing, dance, and act; participating in the arts is what made him happy.

12.

A) Peaceful protests are part of the fabric of America. Protests are only illegal when they become unlawful assemblies or riots.

B) Peaceful protests are part of the fabric of America protests are only illegal when they become unlawful assemblies or riots.

13.

A) While happily at work downtown, Marta's house was burglarized.

B) While Marta was happily at work downtown, her house was burglarized.

14.

A) Officers collected fingerprints on print cards.

B) Fingerprints were collected by officers on print cards.

15.

A) Fran was very afraid, but she kept her fear hidden.

B) Fran was very afraid, but she kept it hidden.

16.

A) The suspect said that her friend took her car.

B) The suspect said that her friend took the suspect's car.

17.

A) Running through the alley, the gun fell from the suspect's waistband.

B) The gun fell from the suspect's waistband as he was running through the alley.

18.

A) Search warrants were issued for three suspects, their accomplices, and their cell phone records.

B) Search warrants were issued for three suspects, the suspects' accomplices, and the suspects' cell phone records.

Vocabulary

Directions: Choose the word that is closest in meaning to the underlined word in the following sentences.

19. Omari felt apathetic in his employment, so he decided to quit his job and go to law school.
    - A) motivated
    - B) dissatisfied
    - C) indifferent
    - D) unsure

20. Hank was drunk and belligerent because his wife left him.
    - A) hostile
    - B) sad
    - C) angry
    - D) loud

21. After years of daily observing people in the worst situations of their lives, Austin's behavior became callous.
    - A) mean
    - B) insensitive
    - C) annoyed
    - D) empathetic

22. Cheryl was nervous, but she did not want to hinder her daughter's dream of becoming a police officer.
    - A) encourage
    - B) expedite
    - C) crush
    - D) impede

23. Clyde was lucid when he told the paramedics who shot him.
    - A) confused
    - B) rational
    - C) emotional
    - D) incomprehensible

24. Larry thought his neighbor, John, was pilfering Larry's morning newspaper, so he reported him to the constable.
    - A) stealing
    - B) borrowing
    - C) moving
    - D) returning

25. Blanca had an inconspicuous scar on her arm from a car accident several years earlier.
    - A) large
    - B) prominent
    - C) unnoticeable
    - D) small

26. After working several twelve-hour shifts in a row, Deputy Nguyen developed a persistent cough.

A) lasting
B) intermittent
C) unrelenting
D) harsh

27. Case law sometimes supersedes legislated law and statutes.

A) supports
B) overrides
C) submits
D) boosts

28. If used successfully, the "heat of passion" defense can mitigate murder to manslaughter.

A) lessen
B) bolster
C) extend
D) change

29. The officers were instructed to write reports that are succinct and not likely to cause confusion.

A) complicated
B) confusing
C) concise
D) long

30. Deputy Wilson worked very hard to hone her skills as an officer.

A) build
B) sharpen
C) steady
D) improve

31. Each year, many laws and statutes are repealed.

A) revoked
B) updated
C) added
D) reworded

32. The evidence shown to the jury was largely circumstantial.

A) illegal
B) incidental
C) irrelevant
D) manufactured

For questions 33-36, choose the word that makes the most sense based on the context of the sentence.

33. The tactical commander outlined the ______ of action for the SWAT team.

A) coarse
B) course

34. The nightly news reported that the police apprehended the ______ killer who had been tormenting River City residents.

A) cereal
B) serial

35. Increased penalties for criminal activity in River City did not appear to have an ______ on the occurrence of crime.

A) effect
B) affect

36. Copper, ______, and titanium components were found in the trunk of the robbery suspect's vehicle.

A) steal
B) steel

Spelling

Directions: Read the following sentences and choose the correct spelling of the missing word.

37. The jury foreman turned ______ the defendant when he read the verdict.

A) tward
B) toword
C) toward
D) tword

38. The District Attorney ______ dropped off the case files this morning.

A) leason
B) liason
C) laison
D) liaison

39. The legislature ______ the law when it was ruled unconstitutional.

A) resinded
B) recinded
C) rescinded
D) resended

40. Even the defendant was ______ when the jury returned a not guilty verdict.

A) surprised
B) suprised
C) supprised
D) surprized

41. Officer Jones had a ______ to speak loudly, which often upset people.

A) tendancy
B) tendency
C) tendencie
D) tendency

42. Officer uses of force are ______ and appropriate actions when suspects fail to comply and can escalate police contacts in a manner that jeopardizes safety.

A) necessary
B) nesisarry
C) necassery
D) necessary

43. John Smith told the court he did not recognize the authority of the ______ and was filing a lawsuit against it to reclaim money owed him as a right of birth.

A) goverment
B) govermant
C) govirnment
D) government

44. Sasha filed a restraining order against her ex-boyfriend because he was ______ her at work.

A) harassing
B) harrassing
C) harasing
D) herassing

45. Pursuant to federal and state laws, all jails and prisons make reasonable ______ for inmates who have disabilities to ensure they have the same or comparable access as inmates who do not have disabilities.

A) acomodations
B) accommodations
C) accommadations
D) accomodations

46. Bystanders were ______ upset after witnessing such a horrific accident.

A) noticably
B) noticibly
C) noticeably
D) noticeabally

47. Jason was arrested because he was in ______ of stolen property.

A) posession
B) possesion
C) possetion
D) possession

48. River City Police Department found itself under ______ after an officer, who was chasing a dangerous criminal, crashed his patrol car into a storefront during business hours.

A) siege
B) seige
C) seege
D) seage

49. At his sentencing, Jim ______ apologized for his role in the home invasion robbery.

A) publicly
B) publicallie
C) publicaly
D) publicely

50. People who are under the influence of certain drugs can become stronger, more unpredictable, and more ______ than an average person.

A) agresive
B) aggresive
C) aggressive
D) agressive

51. Andrea worked long hours as a court reporter and often suffered headaches from extended exposure to ______ lighting.

A) floresent
B) florescint
C) flourescent
D) fluorescent

52. The district attorney and police officer met briefly to review notes prior to the suspect's ______ at the courthouse.

A) arraignment
B) arranement
C) arainment
D) arrangement

53. The suspect claimed to be at the park at the time of the crime, which is a different ______ than the one he provided to the responding officer.

A) alibye
B) aliby
C) alibi
D) allibi

Reading Comprehension

Passage One

When people think critically, they examine, evaluate, and synthesize information they have gathered in order to arrive at a logical conclusion. Critical thinking can be accomplished at a simple or more probing level, depending on whether a cursory or more thoughtful conclusion is desired. At its most basic level, critical thinking is an activity necessary for people to function properly in society. Every day, without thought, most people engage in simple critical thinking exercises as they interact with one another. They observe, analyze, and assess clues and information around them in order to understand others' behavior and to make decisions about how to respond appropriately. When used purposefully, critical thinking can help one gain a much greater understanding of the gathered information. However, many people do not wish to move beyond this basic, instinctual level when deep critical thinking is not

imperative. They do not wish to gain deeper understanding of a person or issue even though gaining such understanding may be as simple as asking, "Why?"

Intensive critical thinking is employed most often in academic settings. Teachers challenge students to apply a higher order of thinking skills to avoid oversimplification, to be objective, and to always ask the next question such as "Why?", "What?", or "What if?" to make reasoned judgments. Critical thinking in academia generally requires a supposition, facts and information, and the ability to infer a logical conclusion from one or more assertions. In academia, critical thinking can either be relegated to mere theoretical dialogue or be applied to an actual problem in order to generate improved conditions.

Since the 1970s, critical thinking has also been used in police work. It is vital, purposeful, and systematic. Police must analyze crimes and criminal activity, establish facts, and determine what information remains unknown. Police investigators analyze patterns and evidence to determine how and why criminal activity was committed and who committed the crime. They ask the questions "What's missing?", "What are the benefits of the crime?", "Who benefited?", "Was the crime planned or opportunistic?" Each question probes deeper into the issue and helps investigators uncover clues to reconstruct other people's reasoning. Critical thinking in police work questions the known facts of a case in such a way that investigators are able to understand criminal actions, and those who commit them, more accurately. Such thinking can help investigators understand a perpetrator's state of mind, determine what the perpetrator was thinking, how he or she was thinking, as well as establish the investigator's opinion of what, how, and why a particular event occurred.

Recently, critical thinking has become even more vital to law enforcement because criminals continue to become more **savvy**. As technology has evolved, so has crime sophistication. Criminals have to work smarter to avoid being apprehended; thus detectives work smarter by studying, evaluating, and assessing evidence to successfully investigate and prosecute criminals.

1. How can the tone of the author best be described?
   A) objective
   B) argumentative
   C) passionate
   D) empathetic

2. As used in paragraph 1, what is the best synonym for imperative:
   A) absolutely necessary
   B) very important
   C) of personal interest
   D) avoidable

3. According to the passage, it can be inferred that the author believes which of the following:
   I. Critical thinking is used in many ways.
   II. Critical thinking is only important in academia.
   III. Critical thinking is vital in police work.

   A) III only
   B) II only
   C) II and III only
   D) I and III only

4. As used in paragraph 4, what is the best definition of savvy?
   A) cool
   B) shrewd
   C) inexperienced
   D) dangerous

5. Which of the following, if true, WEAKENS the main point of paragraph 3?
   A) People do not use critical thinking in everyday life.
   B) Law enforcement began using critical thinking methods in the 1990s.
   C) Academics do not apply theories to real-life situations.
   D) Critical thinking has reduced successful investigations and prosecutions of crimes.

6. Which of the following would be the best title for this passage?
   A) The Definition of Critical Thinking
   B) Critical Thinking and Law Enforcement
   C) The Many Applications of Critical Thinking
   D) Critical Thinking: A Survey

7. According to the passage, what is the main reason for the application of critical thinking in police work?
   A) to help investigators understand criminal activity and criminal perpetrators more accurately
   B) to determine how criminal activity was committed and who committed the crime
   C) because crime sophistication has evolved, and thus investigators must also evolve
   D) all of the above

Passage Two

River City Police Department policy mandates that officers remain in good physical condition while employed with the department. Most officers would gladly comply, but commute times, long work hours, and mandatory overtime account for about fifteen hours of each officer's day. Officers recently asked River City about developing a wellness program for staff members, sworn staff in particular, including the ability to exercise in one of the many gyms located at various River City Police Department's satellite facilities. The resulting memo from the River City chief of police was disseminated to all staff.

"Dear Staff,

It gives me great pleasure to work at an agency that is full of hardworking, motivated individuals, sworn and civilians alike, who seek new ways to continue improving themselves in both professional and personal life.

As you are aware, law enforcement is a physical job that requires the men and women who do the job to maintain a high level of physical fitness. I'm confident all of you would like to maintain that high level of physical fitness. I know this is difficult for many who have family obligations and long commutes from your respective homes in the outlying areas, and for those who work copious overtime shifts. These factors have undoubtedly created barriers for you to reach your personal goals and the required baseline goals of this department.

It was recently brought to my attention that a number of you requested permission to exercise at your duty station during your workday, on your meal break, in one of the various gyms we maintain on facility sites, in order to make exercising easier to fit into your daily routine. I understand your various dilemmas, but for reasons of liability, workers' compensation issues, as well as the logistical issues involved in managing meal breaks so an entire duty station is not working out at the same time, I must deny that request. I will, however, work with you in other ways to help you meet your fitness goals.

As of next week, the following policies will take effect under the River City Police Employee Wellness Pledge program:

- *We will update our meal program for staff members assigned to duty stations where leaving base during shifts is disallowed. We will no longer provide hamburgers, soda, french fries, bacon, or chips. For those of you who work the night shift and eat breakfast, eggs and hash brown potatoes will still be available. If you would like to purchase a soda or snack during your twelve-hour shift, you may do so at the remaining vending machines on-site.*
- *You may not exercise at any gym during duty hours, even if you are on break. You are welcome to work out before or after your assigned shift at any of our gyms.*
- *We will begin a physical fitness club that will meet once a month at one of our facilities for organized workouts. This club is open to the first 30 people who sign up. I, as well as the **warriors** who already work out with me, would love for you to join us at our morning gym sessions.*

Thank you for your diligence to do the job well and to make River City the best police department in the state. I look forward to helping you meet your fitness goals and your feedback on this exciting new program.

Keep up the good work!

Sincerely,

Chief Jeff Hyde"

8. What is the main point of the chief's letter?
   A) Physical fitness is important for police work.
   B) The chief is willing to help officers and staff stay fit.
   C) The chief does not want to be responsible for staff who exercise on duty.
   D) It is primarily the responsibility of the employee to manage time for workouts.

9. According to the chief, what is the main reason he denied the request to work out during work hours?
   A) Staff should be working, not exercising.
   B) Even though staff may be on break, River City is still liable for injuries.
   C) It is difficult logistically to ensure not all staff are working out at the same time.
   D) Both B and C are correct.

10. What is the overall tone of the chief's letter?
   A) cordial
   B) angry
   C) passionate
   D) overbearing

11. What is the best meaning of the word warriors as used in the passage?
- A) a person experienced in warfare
- B) a person who shows great vigor
- C) a person skilled in using weapons
- D) a person with fitness experience

12. According to the passage, how many hours in a given day does the average River City officer have left to eat, sleep, run errands, and work out after working the assigned shift?
- A) fifteen
- B) seventeen
- C) nine
- D) eleven

Passage Three

These days, it is harder than ever for kids to simply "walk away" from a bully. Bullying among children and adolescents has evolved beyond taunting a smaller or less popular kid while he or she is at school, to cyber stalking children across city and state lines with the use of common electronic devices. Because of the increasing reach of bullies, among other factors, suicides and violent confrontations among youth have risen over the years.

Because of the current scope of bullying, school administrators no longer rely solely on teachers to keep kids safe while at school. Rather, administrators build teams of collaborators that include health care workers, teachers, administration, security staff, and law enforcement personnel to ensure schools remain safe places for kids to learn. School resource officers (SROs) receive training in issues that are unique to youth. Generally, SROs have an office on campus. They are stationed at the school and spend their time dealing with law enforcement issues. They also spend a great deal of time talking to kids about anything that interests them, such as school activities, sports, law enforcement, and life in general. Since SROs talk to kids at particular schools regularly, officers are in a unique position to identify emerging issues and prevent them before they develop into greater problems.

SROs play a large role in managing situations that involve bullying so that all involved students and families are heard and respected.

13. Which fact, if true, strengthens the author's main point?
- A) More kids are bullied currently than in previous years.
- B) The majority of bullying happens on school grounds.
- C) Funding for school resource officers has been reduced.
- D) Youth suicides are on the decline.

14. According to the passage, why are SROs important for managing bullying?
- A) SROs arrest students who are too aggressive.
- B) SROs get to know students and can prevent problems.
- C) SROs provide defensive training for victims of bullies.
- D) SROs help teachers learn to identify bullies.

15. According to the passage, why has bullying become so prevalent?
- A) increased negative behavior
- B) school resource officers on school grounds
- C) technological advancement
- D) boredom among children

Passage Four

With over twenty-two million staff members and students on college campuses across the nation, campus security has moved to the spotlight. Security staff have the opportunity to be proactive, educating the college community about campus life and being safe while in a home away from home.

Depending on the size and location of a given school, campus security staffing and scope might be either small-scale or ***monolithically*** *entrenched in the campus community. Additionally, some campuses employ full-time police agencies, while others employ independent contractors or private security companies. However, because the nature and scope of each campus security department varies so widely, the level of communication with other security and law enforcement departments also varies, causing misunderstandings and errors in interdepartmental communication. Now is a crucial time, given the tragic events on school and college campuses and the sheer number of people continually on campuses, to begin creating universal standards so that all students and staff members have the same level of protection regardless of the school where they choose to study or work.*

16. As used in the passage, what is the best definition of the word monolithically?
    A) stonelike
    B) impenetrable
    C) massive
    D) minuscule

17. According to the passage, what types of agencies are employed as campus security?
    A) security companies
    B) law enforcement
    C) contractors
    D) all of the above

18. According to the passage, what is an important problem that needs to be addressed?
    A) communication among agencies
    B) size of security agencies
    C) education of the campus community
    D) universal standards of protection

19. Which of the following, if true, most WEAKENS the argument that the variation in size and scope of campus security departments is the cause of communication problems?
    A) Smaller operations have more money to spend on communications than large ones.
    B) Interoperability between campuses is based on size and scope.
    C) Each operation, regardless of size and scope, uses its own dedicated communication system.
    D) Full-time police agencies have more capabilities than independent contractors.

20. Based on the tone of the passage, it can be inferred that the author believes which statement about campus security?
    A) Campus security operations are varied to the point of dysfunction.
    B) Size and scope do not necessarily matter if the operation functions properly.
    C) Large campus security operations are safer than small ones.
    D) Small campus security operations have better communications capabilities.

Passage Five

State laws determine the age at which persons are automatically charged in adult criminal courts. Persons at or below this age, commonly called the upper age of jurisdiction, are handled in juvenile courts. States may make exceptions, such as for murder or other crimes of violence or evidence of repeated criminal activity, to lower the upper age of jurisdiction. In 2014, New York and North Carolina set the upper age of jurisdiction for juvenile courts at 15, and eight states set the upper age of jurisdiction for juvenile courts at 16. The remaining states set the more reasonable upper age of jurisdiction for juvenile courts at 17, meaning that persons aged 18 or older would be charged in adult criminal courts.

21. What is the main idea of the passage?
    A) Juvenile courts no longer handle any violent crimes committed by minors.
    B) State laws set the age limit for juvenile court jurisdiction, though exceptions exist.
    C) All states agree that 18 is the appropriate age to transfer youth to adult courts.
    D) Youth under the age of 15 are always charged in juvenile courts, regardless of the crime.

22. What can be inferred about the legal treatment of youth offenders across different states?
    A) Youths who commit crimes in all states are tried as adults at age 17.
    B) State laws regarding juvenile jurisdiction are uniform nationwide.
    C) Some states consider the severity or frequency of crimes when determining court jurisdiction.
    D) Juvenile courts in every state will make exceptions for first-time offenders.

23. What is the tone of the passage?
    A) Urgent and emotional
    B) Critical and disapproving
    C) Persuasive and assertive
    D) Analytical and neutral

24. Which of the following sentences from the passage is a claim?
    A) "In 2014, New York and North Carolina set the upper age of jurisdiction for juvenile courts at 15."
    B) "States may make exceptions, such as for murder or other crimes of violence or evidence of repeated criminal activity, to lower the upper age of jurisdiction."
    C) "Persons at or below this age, commonly called the upper age of jurisdiction, are handled in juvenile courts."
    D) "The remaining states set the more reasonable upper age of jurisdiction for juvenile courts at 17."

Answer Explanations #1

Writing

Clarity

1. B: Option A is a run-on sentence.

2. A: Option B contains a vague reference. It is not clear whose supervisor wishes to speak with which employee.

3. A: Option B contains a sentence fragment: "As she made the right turn."

4. B: Option A contains a misplaced modifier. It is not clear if officers who train are caught off guard infrequently, or if officers who train infrequently are caught off guard. Option B is a clearer sentence.

5. A: Option B is a run-on sentence.

6. A: Option B contains a sentence fragment: "Than those who do not unless they are assigned to special covert details that have little contact with ordinary citizens" is not a complete sentence; it is a phrase.

7. B: Option A contains a sentence fragment: "In the leg."

8. A: Option B is a run-on sentence. It requires a semicolon after *common goals*, or the sentence should be broken up into two as in Choice A.

9. B: Choice A contains a misplaced modifier and is unclear. Option A states, "Detective Sherman *almost* got convictions," which implies he got acquittals instead. Option B is clearer, as the word *almost* modifies *every arrest*, rather than *convictions*.

10. A: Option B contains a sentence fragment: "When dealing with family issues."

11. B: Option A contains a vague reference; it is not clear whether singing, dancing, acting, or all three made Kyle happy. Option B is clearer.

12. A: Option B is a run-on sentence. The sentence should be broken up into two, as in Option A, or connected with a semicolon after *America*.

13. B: Option A contains a dangling modifier. The phrase "While happily at work downtown" is modifying "Marta's house" instead of Marta. It appears as if "Marta's house" is "happily at work."

14. A: Option B contains a misplaced modifier. It is not clear whether the officers or the fingerprints are on the print cards. Option A is written more clearly, with *Officers* as the subject and using the active verb *collected*.

15. A: Option B contains a vague reference, using the pronoun *it*. It is not clear what Fran kept hidden. Option A is more clearly written, specifying what Fran kept hidden: "her fear."

16. B: Option A is not clear: did the friend take the suspect's car, or did the friend take her own car? Option B clearly states that the friend took the suspect's car.

17. B: Option A features a dangling, or misplaced, modifier ("Running through the alley"), making it sound like the gun was running through the alley, which is something that is not possible. Option B contains a pronoun (*he*) that follows its antecedent (*the suspect*), making it clear that the suspect was running through the alley.

18. B: In Option A, it is unclear as to whose cell phone records the search warrant is for: is it for the suspect's cell phone records, the accomplices' cell phone records, or both the suspect's and accomplices' records? Option B makes it clear that the search warrant is for the suspect's cell phone records.

Vocabulary

19. C: *Apathetic* means *indifferent.* Omari might also be unsatisfied with his work, but *dissatisfied* is not the best answer here. He is the opposite of *motivated.* If he were *unsure* about his work, he might not be so quick to leave it.

20. A: *Belligerent* means *hostile*. The other Options—*sad, angry,* and *loud*—are not the best answers because a person may exhibit any of those characteristics without being hostile or combative.

21. B: *Callous* means *insensitive.* A person may be *mean* or *annoyed* without being insensitive, so Options A and C are not the best. Option D— *empathetic*—means the opposite of *callous* or *insensitive*.

22. D: To *hinder* means to *impede*. To *impede* is less severe than to *crush*, which is to destroy something. Both *encourage* and *expedite* imply helping something to happen, which is the opposite meaning of *hinder*.

23. B: *Lucid* means *rational* or *clear*. Options A and D—*confused* and *incomprehensible*—are the opposite of *rational*. Clyde may have been *emotional*, but that does not explain why he was able to describe a person while in a stressful situation.

24. A: *Pilfering* means *stealing*. If John had been *borrowing, moving,* or *returning* the newspaper, it is unlikely that Larry would have taken such drastic action.

25. C: *Inconspicuous* means *unnoticeable*. Option B, *prominent*, means the opposite. Options A and D—*large* and *small*—are not the best options because both large and small items could be inconspicuous.

26. B: *Intermittent* is the opposite of *persistent*. Options A and C, *lasting* and *unrelenting*, are synonyms. *Harsh* is unconnected because both an intermittent and a persistent cough could be harsh.

27. C: *Submits* is the opposite of *supersede. Overrides* is a synonym for *supersedes. Supports* and *boosts* are closer in meaning to *supersedes*, though not exactly the same, as they fail to imply the sense of overruling; in any case, they are not opposite in meaning to *supersedes*.

28. B: *Bolster* is the opposite of *mitigate*. Option A, *lessen*, is a synonym. The other options, *extend* and *change*, do not relate to *mitigate*.

29. C: *Succinct* means *concise*, which means *brief.* The other options all have the opposite meaning of *concise*.

30. B: To *hone* is to *sharpen. Build* and *improve* are close in meaning to *hone* but are not synonyms. *Steady* is unrelated.

31. A: *Repealed* means *revoked. Updated, added,* and *reworded* would imply the opposite.

32. B: Something that is described as *circumstantial* is *incidental*; in other words, it is not intentional or calculated. Using context clues, you can eliminate Option A (*illegal*): if evidence is illegal, it almost certainly would not be made available to a jury; the same logic applies to Option C (*irrelevant*). While *manufactured* (Option D) could be tempting to choose, it is not the definition of *circumstantial*.

33. B: In this context, *course* means "manner of procedure." *Coarse* is a homonym and means "harsh" or "grating."

34. B: In this context, *serial* means "producing a series of similar actions," such as killing. *Cereal* is an edible grain.

35. A: *Effect* as used in this context is a noun. Generally (though there are exceptions), the word *affect* is a verb, and *effect* is a noun. To *affect* is to "act upon something to cause change," as in "The snow *affected* his ability to drive." An *effect* is a result, as in "The snow had a negative *effect* on the undercarriage of his car." In the exam question, the "increased penalties" had no *effect* on crime.

36. B: *Steel* is a type of metal and therefore fits best in the blank, which appears as part of a series of different types of metals that are being listed. *Steal* is a verb that means to take something that belongs to someone else.

Spelling

37. C: Option C, *toward*, is spelled correctly.

38. D: Option D, *liaison*, is spelled correctly.

39. C: Option C, *rescinded*, is spelled correctly.

40. A: Option A, *surprised*, is spelled correctly.

41. B: Option B, *tendency*, is spelled correctly.

42. A: Option A, *necessary*, is spelled correctly.

43. D: Option D, *government*, is spelled correctly.

44. A: Option A, *harassing*, is spelled correctly.

45. B: Option B, *accommodations*, is spelled correctly.

46. C: Option C, *noticeably*, is spelled correctly.

47. D: Option D, *possession*, is spelled correctly.

48. A: Option A, *siege*, is spelled correctly.

49. A: Option A, *publicly*, is spelled correctly.

50. C: Option C, *aggressive*, is spelled correctly.

51. D: Option D, *fluorescent*, is spelled correctly.

52. A: Option A, *arraignment*, is spelled correctly.

53. C: Option C, *alibi*, is spelled correctly.

Reading Comprehension

1. A: The passage is written with an impersonal objective tone, much like an article or news report; it is not written to persuade or debate, nor is it argumentative, passionate, or empathetic.

2. A: In this context, *imperative* means "absolutely necessary." The passage asserts that "many people do not wish to move beyond this basic, instinctual level" of thought to critical thinking unless they must. It must therefore be essential—not just important or interesting—for them to engage in critical thinking (Options B and C). Option D, *avoidable*, is not relevant here.

3. D: Only I and III are true. Choice II, which states critical thinking is *only* important in academia, contradicts the first sentence of paragraph 3: "Since the 1970s, critical thinking has also been used in police work." In fact, the point of the passage is that critical thinking is vital to police work (Choice III).

4. B: The definition of *savvy* is *shrewd*. This paragraph states that policing requires critical thinking to outsmart criminals. Option A, *cool*, is not relevant here. *Inexperienced* has the opposite meaning; a savvy criminal would likely be quite experienced. And *dangerous* criminals are not necessarily savvy.

5. D: If fewer crimes were successfully investigated and prosecuted since police began using critical thinking in investigations, then it would appear critical thinking is not helpful in police work. The purpose of paragraph 3 is to illustrate the many ways in which critical thinking has been used and can help in law enforcement. Options A, B, and C are incorrect because they misstate facts or ideas from the passage.

6. B: The best title for this passage is "Critical Thinking and Law Enforcement." Although the passage defines critical thinking and illustrates its various applications, the bulk of the passage talks about the application of critical thinking to law enforcement. Thus, Option B is the best option.

7. D: Each point was presented as an important reason for which critical thinking is used in law enforcement.

8. D: The chief's letter identifies personal reasons why many people cannot schedule exercise into their daily routines. It also mentions the "warriors" who do work out in the morning, and the liability issues around allowing staff to exercise during shifts. Thus, Option D is the best answer; the chief will help, but he puts the responsibility on the employee to manage his or her time.

9. D: The chief notes both logistics and liability as reasons why he denied the request.

10. A: The tone of the letter is cordial. The letter uses mostly friendly and supportive words in a professional format. The chief begins his letter by applauding employees for wanting to meet standards. He clearly explains the reasoning for his own choices in changing policy by taking away food options and prohibiting exercise on meal breaks. While it is debatable whether those choices are good policies for the officers, the tone of the letter is not angry or overbearing, ruling out Options B and D. The chief does express enthusiasm for the "warriors" he already works out with and says they would "love" other officers to join them, but this is more enthusiastic than overbearing, ruling out Option C.

11. B: As used in the passage, the chief implies the "warriors" who work out every morning with him show motivation, energy, and a willingness to do what it takes to fit exercise into their schedules. Warfare and weapons are irrelevant to this passage. Finally, the chief does not suggest that those who work out with him are exceptionally experienced; otherwise, he would not invite those officers who are looking to improve their fitness to join them.

12. C: The introduction to the passage states that most officers spend fifteen hours a day working and commuting. There are twenty-four hours in a day; fifteen subtracted from twenty-four leaves nine hours remaining.

13. A: The author's main point is that bullying has increased in scope from years past. If the number of children being bullied has increased, this strengthens the author's argument. The author asserts that bullying occurs beyond school, thanks to technology, making Option B incorrect. The passage discusses SROs at length, so if there were less funding for SROs, the argument would be weakened, making Option C incorrect. Finally, Option D directly contradicts the passage, which states that youth suicides are increasing.

14. B: According to the passage, "SROs talk to kids at particular schools regularly," so "officers are in a unique position to identify emerging issues and prevent them before they develop into greater problems." The passage never states that SROs arrest bullies, just that SROs "are stationed at the school and spend their time dealing with law enforcement issues." SROs do not offer training; they "receive training in issues that are unique to youth." The passage never states specifically that SROs show teachers how to identify bullies, just that all personnel work together "to ensure schools remain safe places for kids to learn."

15. C: The passage immediately asserts that technological advancement has made bullying more prevalent. The first paragraph states that "bullying among children and adolescents has evolved . . . to cyber stalking children across city and state lines with the use of common electronic devices." The passage explains that school resource officers enhance safety at school, so Option B is not correct. Finally, the passage never mentions more negative behavior among children or boredom as factors in bullying, ruling out Options A and D.

16. C: *Monolithically* means *massively*. It can also mean *stonelike*, but in this context, Option C is the better answer since the passage suggests that the agency is massive in contrast to "small-scale." This comparison makes Option C better than Option B, *impenetrable*. *Minuscule*, Option D, means the opposite.

17. D: The passage mentions security companies, law enforcement, and contractors as agencies employed as campus security.

18. A: According to the passage, "[b]ecause the nature and scope of each campus security department varies so widely, the level of communication with other security and law enforcement departments also varies, causing misunderstandings and errors in interdepartmental communication." The passage mentions the type and size of various security agencies as a reason communication is a problem, but the overarching problem is communication, so Option A is a better answer than Option B. The passage states that "educating the college community about campus life and being safe while in a home away from home" is the job of campus security, not a problem, making Option C incorrect. Finally, the author suggests "to begin creating universal standards" for protection. Universal standards are not problems but rather are possible solutions to problems.

19. C: The passage mentions that the varying size and scope of different agencies make it difficult for them to communicate with one another. If each agency used its own dedicated communication system, then these communication systems would be the reason for interagency communication problems rather than the variation in size and scope of the agencies. Options A, B, and D support the author's argument, because they assert that the ability of an agency to communicate effectively is based on its size.

20. B: The author does not make a judgment about any specific type of security agency. Therefore, it can be inferred from the passage that the author believes that size and scope of a security department or operation do not matter as long as the operation functions properly.

21. B: The primary idea in the passage is related to how state laws set the age limit for juvenile court jurisdiction. Option A is incorrect because juvenile courts may still handle violent crimes committed by minors, depending on the state and circumstances. Option C is wrong because states do not universally agree on 18 as the age to transfer youth to adult courts. Option D is wrong because some youth under age 15 may still be charged in adult court under certain exceptions.

22. C: The passage indicates that states differ in their approaches to determining court jurisdiction. Option A is incorrect because not all states try youths as adults at age 17. Option B is incorrect because juvenile jurisdiction laws are not uniform across the country. Option D is incorrect because the passage does not state that all states make exceptions for first-time offenders.

23. D: The passage has an analytical and neutral tone because it impartially states facts about its subject. Option A is incorrect because the passage does not use emotional or urgent language. Option B is incorrect because the tone is neither critical nor disapproving but rather factual and objective. Option C is incorrect because the passage is not trying to persuade or argue a position.

24. D: In the passage, the phrase "the more reasonable age" is an opinion. Option A is incorrect because it is a factual statement about specific states. Option B is incorrect because it describes policy exceptions; it does not make a general claim. Option C is incorrect because it presents a fact, not an assertion or opinion.

Practice Test #2

Writing

Clarity

Directions: In the following sentence pairs, identify the sentence that is most clearly written.

1.
   A) The bus driver lost control of the bus while turning a corner. Too fast.
   B) The bus driver lost control of the bus while turning a corner too fast.

2.
   A) Steven saw his stolen car on the way to work.
   B) On the way to work, Steven saw his stolen car.

3.
   A) Jared drank several alcoholic beverages at the party. He crashed into a parked car on the way home and was arrested for DUI.
   B) Jared drank several alcoholic beverages at the party he crashed into a parked car on the way home and was arrested for DUI.

4.
   A) Officer Daryn said he did not like to drive in pursuits because the fast speeds make you sick.
   B) Officer Daryn said he did not like to drive in pursuits because the fast speeds make him sick.

5.
   A) Generally, most people remain unaware of the judicial system's process. Unless they become a party to an action.
   B) Generally, most people remain unaware of the judicial system's process unless they become a party to an action.

6.
   A) As the defendant was remanded into custody, the judge lectured him.
   B) The judge lectured the defendant as he was remanded into custody.

7.
   A) Court clerks are essential members of the court staff they maintain all the court documents and record each word spoken in court while "on the record."
   B) Court clerks are essential members of the court staff. They maintain all the court documents and record each word spoken in court while "on the record."

8.
   A) Jack called the Sheriff's Office, but they did not return his call.
   B) Jack called the Sheriff's Office, but the answering service did not return his call.

9.
  A) Greg's neighbor has a dog. That barks all hours of the day and night.
  B) Greg's neighbor has a dog that barks all hours of the day and night.

10.
  A) Officer Martinez reported the stolen car.
  B) The car was reported stolen by Officer Martinez.

11.
  A) Community policing is not a new concept it has, however, recently received a face-lift.
  B) Community policing is not a new concept. It has, however, recently received a face-lift.

12.
  A) Eagerly awaiting time off, Ebony's vacation was just about to start.
  B) Eagerly awaiting time off, Ebony was just about to start her vacation.

13.
  A) Stoplights are often timed for safety when drivers "jump" the green, they are cheating the system, and the results could be deadly.
  B) Stoplights are often timed for safety. When drivers "jump" the green, they are cheating the system, and the results could be deadly.

14.
  A) Inmates received lunches in bags from deputies.
  B) Inmates received lunches from deputies in bags.

15.
  A) Every time Alonzo turned on the TV, they said another city was experiencing unrest.
  B) Every time Alonzo turned on the TV, the news reported another city was experiencing unrest.

16.
  A) The suspects were unaware that the agents had fixed security cameras on them.
  B) The agents had fixed security cameras on the suspects, who were unaware.

17.
  A) Over a dozen witnesses came forward. To describe what they had seen.
  B) Over a dozen witnesses came forward to describe what they had seen.

Vocabulary

Directions: Choose the word that is closest in meaning to the underlined word in the following sentences.

18. Julian became <u>frantic</u> when he realized his child was missing.
  A) frenzied
  B) calm
  C) frustrated
  D) upset

19. Henry only exacerbated the problem when he poured water on a grease fire.
A) hurt
B) reduced
C) aggravated
D) excited

20. Deputy Hanes writes reports that tend to be verbose.
A) concise
B) clear
C) confusing
D) wordy

21. One purpose of community policing is to foster relationships between the police and the communities they serve.
A) alleviate
B) create
C) discourage
D) promote

22. It is impossible to quantify the damage resulting from the fire.
A) measure
B) understand
C) extend
D) improve

23. The jury came to a dubious conclusion based on the evidence.
A) dishonest
B) questionable
C) obvious
D) definite

24. Officers furtively infiltrated the gang in order to gather intelligence.
A) stealthily
B) fraudulently
C) brazenly
D) openly

25. The couple told the officer that, although they were shouting at each other, they were not quarreling.
A) boxing
B) speaking
C) playing
D) arguing

26. Some criminals manage to have an affable demeanor despite the atrocity of their crimes.
A) warm
B) friendly
C) angry
D) wonderful

27. Sally <u>alienated</u> all her family and friends when she became addicted to drugs.

A) angered
B) estranged
C) frustrated
D) united

28. The suspect said he was at work at the time of the crime, and his supervisor <u>corroborated</u> this alibi.

A) refuted
B) argued
C) supported
D) denied

Directions: Choose a word from the answer options that is the best antonym of the underlined word.

29. Judge Singleton <u>abdicated</u> her seat on the bench because she was seriously ill.

A) left
B) maintained
C) abandoned
D) relinquished

30. The jury was admonished and advised that they could not <u>deviate</u> from the instructions.

A) diverge
B) depart
C) sway
D) remain

31. Toby made his way to the top with <u>guile</u> and swindled thousands of people out of millions of dollars.

A) duplicity
B) assistance
C) honesty
D) savvy

Directions: Choose the word that makes the most sense based on the context of the sentence.

32. When Tom spoke at the town hall meeting, he intended his words to motivate people to fight for their rights, not to __________ a riot.

A) incite
B) insight

33. Mayor Brighton did not __________ whether Oscar's speech was protected by the First Amendment of the Constitution.

A) know
B) no

34. Jerry had not eaten in four days and had no money, so he decided to __________ some food to get by.

A) steel
B) steal

35. Recent budget cuts prompted the department to _________ down the number of overtime hours allowed.

A) pare
B) pair

Spelling

Directions: Read the following sentences and choose the correct spelling of the missing word.

36. The relationship of the prosecution and the defense is _______ by design.

A) adversarial
B) advirsarial
C) advirsareal
D) adverserial

37. The judge ruled the information was not ________ to the case and was thus inadmissible.

A) germain
B) germean
C) girmain
D) germane

38. The tension in the courtroom was _______ as the jury prepared to read the verdict.

A) palpible
B) palpable
C) palpebal
D) palpabal

39. The judge signed a _______ to compel the company to turn the phone records over to the police.

A) supena
B) suppena
C) subpoena
D) supeana

40. Judy was _______ of her son, who suddenly had a lot of money and rarely came home at night.

A) suspisious
B) suspisios
C) suspiscious
D) suspicious

41. At the scene of a car accident, Officer Garcia attempted to _______ the exchange of information between drivers because they were arguing with each other.

A) fasilitate
B) fascilitate
C) facilitate
D) facilatate

42. The suspect was _______ for four hours before he confessed.

A) interrogated
B) interogated
C) interragated
D) interagated

43. Four _______ witnesses placed Harry at the scene of the crime.

A) indapendant
B) independent
C) independant
D) indapendent

44. As a victim of a _______ crime, Luis devoted his time to changing legislation regarding victims' rights.

A) heinous
B) hanous
C) haneous
D) hienous

45. Gabriel was an _______ child who would not listen to his parents and continued to get into trouble.

A) incorrigable
B) inccorigable
C) incorrigeable
D) incorrigible

46. Officer Sasser knew the importance of attention to detail and never performed her duties in a _______ manner.

A) perfunctary
B) perfunctory
C) perfunctiry
D) perfunctery

47. Sovereign citizens are people who belong to a _______ organization and refuse to recognize the authority of the United States.

A) seditious
B) seditiuos
C) saditious
D) siditious

48. The president of the neighborhood watch called the police and requested a house be placed under _______ because its occupants were suspected of drug dealing.

A) survailance
B) surveillance
C) survielance
D) servielance

49. Stella survived her attack because she was _______.

A) tenacious
B) tinasious
C) tenasious
D) tanancious

50. Ed was arrested for _______ because he was drunk and sleeping on a park bench at two o'clock in the afternoon.

A) vagrency
B) vagrincie
C) vagrincy
D) vagrancy

Reading Comprehension

Passage One

Since the police usually do not have the opportunity to watch a crime as it happens, they must rely on evidence, statements from witnesses and involved parties, and deduction skills to draw conclusions about what actually occurred. Although reliance on information from others is essential, the information officers receive is often inaccurate either because the individual was mistaken in his or her perception, was biased, or was purposefully deceptive. Police must skillfully sift through all of the information they receive and decide which is accurate and which is not. The officer's decision is generally based on his or her assessment of the information's source and whether it is credible or reliable. There are three main reasons information is unreliable.

The most frequent type of unreliable information is mistaken perception. Mistaken perception happens when otherwise honest and reliable people give information they believe to be true but is not. Mistaken perception can happen for a number of reasons. For example, during a stressful situation the brain releases adrenaline into the body, causing physiological changes. During periods of extreme stress, blood rushes away from nonessential organs and systems toward the heart. As this happens, people often experience various sensory disturbances, such as time anomalies. Often witnesses and involved parties will report that a greater or lesser amount of time passed than actually did. A time ***anomaly*** *affects an individual's sense of time, which appears to be moving at lightning speed or in slow motion. Sight and sound may also be affected. Witnesses and involved parties experiencing auditory occlusion often describe a temporary loss or lessening of hearing; sounds are muted or unheard. People also experience the feeling of tunnel vision, wherein peripheral vision is diminished and they can only see what is directly in front of them. People who undergo these physiological changes, even when mild, may have a distorted perception of the incident even though they are telling the truth based on their recollection. Police officers must pay attention to behavior cues that signal an individual may have altered perception due to physiological disturbances.*

Another issue with involved party reliability is individual bias. While some people have biases they are aware of, sometimes people have biases they are unaware of for a number of reasons. The bias may stem from accepting another source of information as true without question. In other words, the individual was uncritical of the information received and then passed along to police. People also may have a bias due to a vested interest in a particular view or outcome, and their perception is altered by that interest. Police officers must be diligent in identifying any possible biases during the interview process when establishing witness accuracy and reliability.

Lastly, there are times when people are simply dishonest. The reason for their dishonesty may have nothing to do with the situation at hand. The motivation for the dishonesty may or may not be relevant to the incident, but it is crucial when determining the reliability of the statement itself. If a person is willing to be dishonest to the police, for whatever reason, his or her credibility must also be called into question. Police officers must pay attention to accounts of an incident by witnesses and involved parties for inconsistencies and ***blatant*** *misinformation.*

There are many reasons why accounts of an incident by witnesses and involved parties might be unreliable. It is the officer's duty to use critical thinking, deduction, and logical reasoning to determine what is or is not reliable and why. Police officers have a variety of tools at their disposals in order to determine the accuracy of witness or involved party statements. Corroboration, witness expertise, police officer observations, evidence located at the scene, and the like, can help an officer analyze the information to determine the probable reliability of a statement.

1. What is the main point of this article?
   A) Witnesses are dishonest.
   B) Witnesses can be unreliable.
   C) Stress can alter witnesses' perception.
   D) Biased witnesses are unreliable.

2. The passage implies which one of the following?
   A) Because witnesses are often unreliable, officers must be diligent in their investigation.
   B) Witnesses are never reliable; officers must use other evidence to prove crimes.
   C) The most frequent type of unreliable information is individual bias.
   D) Only some witnesses should be trusted, but it is impossible to tell who is reliable.

3. According to this article, what is the main reason for problems with witness reliability?
   A) dishonesty
   B) mistaken perception
   C) bias
   D) all of the above

4. According to the passage, which of the following is true?
   A) People only lie for reasons related to the situation.
   B) Some people are unaware of bias they hold.
   C) During high-stress situations, blood rushes away from the heart.
   D) Witnesses' perception of time is generally quite accurate.

5. According to the passage, what is auditory occlusion?
   A) total loss of hearing
   B) tunnel vision
   C) a temporary loss or lessening of hearing
   D) a sensory disturbance

6. What is the best synonym for the word *anomaly* as it is used in paragraph 2 of the passage?
   A) commonality
   B) ambivalence
   C) abnormality
   D) uncertainty

7. What word below is the best meaning of the word *blatant* as it is used in paragraph 4 of the passage?
   A) obvious
   B) flagrant
   C) subtle
   D) implied

Passage Two

Think cattle rustling is a thing of the past? Think again. As of March 2014, cattle rustling in the western United States is still "a thing." Ranchers and law enforcement are ***diligently*** *working together to protect herds and keep them safe from a brand-new threat—meth addicts. People addicted to methamphetamine have turned in their climbing boots and copper wire–grabbing gloves to steal cows in order to finance their drug habits. Where's the Outlaw Josey Wales when you need him?*

Levity aside, neither of the aforementioned issues is a laughing matter. Methamphetamine addiction is very serious, dangerous, and expensive to maintain. Issues surrounding the crime of cow theft is equally serious, dangerous, and expensive. Cows are valuable and can be sold at auction for around $1,000 a head. A local news station obtained video depicting thieves as they stole an entire pen of cows by coaxing them into the back of a big rig in the middle of the night. Another rancher had 100 cows stolen. At $1,000 a head, that's big money—and big jail time. Currently, cattle rustling carries penalties of up to ten years in prison. The problem for ranchers, while fortuitous for the thieves, is that it's fairly easy to avoid detection while selling stolen livestock at auction. Why? The cows often are not branded.

Why not simply brand the cows? Well, that depends on the rancher. Some ranchers seek support and endorsements from the Certified Humane Project (CHP), and organizations like it, for meat products. CHP grades livestock on a step level from 1 to 5, with 1 being the lowest and 5 being the highest. The higher the meat's rating, the more natural, healthy, and flavorful it is, allowing the farmer to command a premium price. As farmers desire to return to natural and humane ways of farming and cattle raising, while also increasing their earnings potential, fewer farmers are branding their cattle. If farmers treat their animals humanely and get their animals' habitat closer to what normally occurs in nature, the meat will have a higher rating when it finally makes it to the grocery stores.

One thing CHP has noted is that branding animals is not humane. As such, ranchers have a decision to make: protect the herd with brands or resist branding to achieve higher CHP step ratings. Either choice will likely cost the ranchers big bucks.

8. What is the main point of this passage?
   A) Cows are expensive.
   B) Cattle rustling is still a big problem for ranchers.
   C) Ranchers should brand their cows.
   D) Meat certifications are big money.

9. In paragraph 2, a rancher is said to have had 100 cows stolen. According to the article, what is the total monetary loss of the cows before processing?

A) $1,000,000
B) $10,000
C) $100,000
D) $1,000

10. According to the passage, what is a service that Certified Humane Project (CHP) provides?

A) third-party evaluation of farms and animal habitat
B) rate livestock and resultant meat products
C) create benchmarks for organic humane food sources
D) all of the above

11. The passage implies that which one of the following is true about branding?

A) Branding does not affect the animals.
B) Branding is not a major issue for ranchers.
C) Ranchers make more money if they don't brand.
D) Most ranchers brand their cattle.

12. Which one of the following does the passage not mention?

A) Josey Wales, the outlaw
B) cattle rustling as "big money" for meth addicts
C) copper as a source for addicts to fund their habits
D) services for addicts to overcome addiction

13. Which of the words below most closely matches the meaning of the word *diligently* as used in the first paragraph?

A) neglectful
B) persistently
C) unconcerned
D) carefully

14. Which of the following is a central dilemma for ranchers?

A) It's easy to sell stolen cattle undetected because they are not branded, but branding the animals reduces their value.
B) Ranchers often know the addicts who steal their cattle because they are community and family members, making it difficult to prosecute them.
C) Branding cattle increases the value of the meat on the market, but it hurts the cows and is not humane.
D) The Certified Humane Project has been advocating to reduce meat consumption, making it difficult to sell beef.

Passage Three

After a person convicted of a crime has served a sentence in a jail or prison, he or she is released back into the community. Prisoner release is a source of relief or frustration depending on individual perceptions, experience, and expectations. Some people believe a person who has committed a crime is lost and can never be ***redeemed****. Others believe there are justifiable reasons why any given crime was committed, and thus very few people should go to jail or prison for extended times. Regardless of one's* *position, when a person has served a sentence, that individual will be released and will return to the community. Moreover, regardless of the opinions of others, the released person often has to deal with fear, confusion, and apprehension.*

So there are many questions that arise. Is it the responsibility of the community to support people who have violated the public trust as they re-enter society? And if so, how do communities support people newly released from jail so they do not become statistics of recidivism? The answer to these questions forms the basis of re-entry programs throughout the nation.

Generally speaking, most re-entry programs are composed of various community members and stakeholders. Collaboration between probation, parole, law enforcement, medical and mental health care workers, employment services, housing advocates, clergy, and a host of other services including substance abuse and domestic violence counseling are essential for making the transition smooth and successful. Collaborative partners ensure that resources are set up, or in motion, by the time of release so that participants do not find themselves homeless or re-entering a detrimental living situation immediately upon leaving prison.

Re-entry programs have shown success in many communities; however, the perceived level of success may be well above or well below expectations, depending on individual ***disposition****, the attitude of the participant, and the community in which they now live.*

15. Based on the tone of this passage, what is the purpose of the passage?
   A) to persuade
   B) to share information
   C) to admonish
   D) to stimulate thought

16. What is an appropriate title for this passage?
   A) Community Frustrated over Prisoner Release
   B) Prisoner Re-entry Programs: What Happens Next
   C) How to Decrease Recidivism Rates
   D) Prisoner Re-entry

17. Based on the passage, it can be inferred that the author believes which one of the following?
   A) Criminals should never be let out of prison.
   B) Many crimes are justified, and fewer people should receive long prison terms.
   C) Community involvement is important for re-entry programs to work well.
   D) Re-entry programs work.

18. As used in the last sentence, what is the best definition of the word *disposition*?
   A) bad attitude
   B) frustrations
   C) positivity
   D) natural inclination

19. What is the purpose of the second paragraph?
   A) to illustrate the depth of the issue
   B) to offer a supporting example
   C) to avoid taking a position
   D) to provide more details about the main idea

20. Which is the best synonym for the word *redeemed* as used in paragraph 1?
   A) exchanged
   B) converted
   C) reformed
   D) reclaimed

Passage Four

An estimated 5,407,300 persons were under the supervision of adult correctional systems in the United States at year-end 2022, and 3,668,800 of those were under community supervision, according to Correctional Populations in the United States, 2022. The adult correctional system is responsible for all correctional supervision in the United States, including both persons incarcerated in prisons and jails and persons supervised in the community on probation and parole. About 1 in 48 adult US residents (2 percent) were under correctional supervision at the end of 2022. More than two-thirds (3,668,800) of persons under correctional supervision were on probation or parole and supervised by competent probation officers in the community, while almost one-third (1,827,600) were incarcerated in state or federal prisons or local jails.

21. What can be inferred about the US adult correctional system based on the statistics provided in the passage?
   A) The majority of adults under correctional supervision are incarcerated in prisons or jails.
   B) Most persons under correctional supervision are monitored in the community rather than in correctional facilities.
   C) The percentage of adults under correctional supervision has significantly increased in recent years.
   D) Only a small proportion of adults under correctional supervision in the US are subject to probation or parole.

22. What is the main idea of the passage?
   A) The majority of people under correctional supervision in the US are incarcerated in prisons and jails.
   B) Probation and parole are becoming less common forms of correctional supervision in the correctional system.
   C) Most adults under correctional supervision in the US are managed in the community rather than incarcerated.
   D) The correctional system in the US has not changed significantly over the past decade.

23. How is the passage structured?
   A) by comparing two opposing viewpoints about incarceration
   B) by presenting a general overview supported by statistical evidence
   C) by narrating a sequence of events in the correctional system's history
   D) by describing a problem and offering potential solutions

24. Which of the following sentences from the passage is a claim?

A) "The adult correctional system is responsible for all correctional supervision in the United States, including both persons incarcerated in prisons and jails and persons supervised in the community on probation and parole."

B) "An estimated 5,407,300 persons were under the supervision of adult correctional systems in the United States at year-end 2022."

C) "More than two-thirds of persons under correctional supervision were supervised by competent probation officers in the community on probation or parole."

D) "About 1 in 48 adult US residents (2 percent) were under correctional supervision at the end of 2022."

Answer Explanations #2

Writing

Clarity

1. B: Option A contains a sentence fragment ("Too fast").

2. B: Option A contains a misplaced modifier: "on the way to work." It appears as though Steven's car, not Steven, is "on the way to work."

3. A: Option B is a run-on sentence requiring punctuation after "party."

4. B: Option A contains a vague reference. Officer Daryn says he does not like to drive fast but references an unspecified "you" in the sentence. Option B clearly states that it is Officer Daryn who gets sick at high speeds.

5. B: Option A contains a sentence fragment. "Unless they become a party to an action" is a dependent clause and must be connected to the preceding sentence with punctuation.

6. A: Option B contains a vague reference: "he." It is unclear whether the judge or the defendant was remanded into custody.

7. B: Option A is a run-on sentence. A semicolon is required after "staff," or a period should be inserted and a new sentence begun, as in Option B.

8. B: Option A contains a vague reference. Jack calls the Sheriff's Office, which is a business comprised of more than one person but is itself a singular unit; therefore, the use of the pronoun "they" is improper. Option B is clearer.

9. B: Option A contains a sentence fragment. The phrase "That barks all hours of the day and night" is dependent on the sentence "Greg's neighbor has a dog."

10. A: Option B contains a misplaced modifier: the phrase "by Officer Martinez." As written, it appears that Officer Martinez stole the car. Option A is written more clearly to show that Officer Martinez made the report.

11. B: Option A is a run-on sentence requiring punctuation after "concept."

12. B: Option A contains a misplaced modifier. The phrase "eagerly awaiting time off" is a dangling modifier modifying "Ebony's vacation" rather than "Ebony," making it appear that the vacation, not the person, was waiting for time off.

13. B: Option A is a run-on sentence. Punctuation is required after "safety."

14. A: Option B contains a misplaced modifier: "in bags." It is unclear whether the lunches or the deputies were in bags.

15. B: Option A contains a vague reference. It is unclear to whom "they" refers. This sentence illustrates an improper use of the pronoun "they."

16. B: The use of the pronoun *them* in Option A is unclear: do the agents have security cameras fixed on them, or do the suspects have security cameras fixed on them? Option B makes it clear that the agents fixed the security cameras on the suspects.

17. B: Option A contains a sentence fragment ("To describe what they had seen.") Option B is grammatically sound and written more clearly.

Vocabulary

18. A: *Frantic* means *frenzied.* Option B, *calm*, is the opposite of *frantic*; it is unlikely a father would be calm if he realized his child was missing. Options C and D—*frustrated* and *upset*—are both incorrect because it is possible to be frustrated or upset without being frantic.

19. C: *Exacerbated* means *aggravated*, to make something worse. Option A, *hurt*, is not relevant here; it is not possible to "hurt" a problem. Option B, *reduced*, means the opposite of *exacerbated*. Option D, *excited*, lacks the negative connotation of *exacerbated*.

20. D: *Verbose* means *wordy*. *Concise* is the opposite of *wordy*. Options B and C, *clear* and *confusing*, are not the best options because a text can be clear or confusing while being verbose at the same time.

21. D: To *foster* means to *promote*. Option B, *create*, is incorrect because it implies the relationships do not yet exist. Options A and C, *alleviate* and *discourage*, imply the opposite of *promote*.

22. A: To *quantify* is to *measure* or count the value of something. Quantifying something might make it more *understandable*, but Option A, *measure*, is the best answer here.

23. B: *Dubious* means *questionable*. *Dishonest*, Option A, is not the same as *dubious*; something can be questionable while still being the truth. Option C, *obvious*, is unrelated in meaning. Option D, *definite*, implies certainty, the opposite of *dubious*.

24. A: *Furtively* means *stealthily*. *Fraudulently*, Option B, is unrelated. Options C and D, *brazenly* and *openly*, are antonyms of *furtively*.

25. D: *Quarreling* means *arguing*; it implies a verbal confrontation. While Option A could be tempting to choose, it is not closest in meaning to the word *quarrel*. While Option B (*speaking*) might also be a tempting option, it also does not fit the definition of *quarrel* as closely as *arguing*; the context clue "although they were shouting" also signals that the couple is arguing and not merely speaking. Option C (*playing*) is not related to the idea of *quarreling*.

26. B: *Affable* means *friendly*. *Friendly* is a more accurate meaning than *warm*, Option A. *Angry*, Option C, would imply unfriendly, the opposite. *Wonderful*, while positive, is not the same as *friendly*.

27. B: *Alienated* means *estranged*. It is likely that her family was also *angered* and *frustrated*, but Options A and C are incorrect because one can be angry and frustrated with a person while still maintaining a relationship with that person. Option D, *united*, is an antonym of *alienated*.

28. C: *Supported* is the best synonym for the word *corroborated*. The other options are all antonyms of the word *corroborated*.

29. B: *Abdicated* is an antonym of *maintained*. Option D, *relinquished*, is a synonym. Option A, *left*, lacks the implication of a responsible departure; when relinquishing a position, the office holder gives it up to another. Likewise, Option C, *abandoned*, is close in meaning but overly extreme; someone can *relinquish* a position or role without leaving irresponsibly.

30. D: *Deviate* is the opposite of *remain*. The other options—*diverge*, *depart*, and *sway*—are synonyms of *diverge*.

31. C: *Guile* is the opposite of *hones- ty*. Option A, *duplicity*, is a synonym. *Assistance*, Option B, is unrelated in meaning and does not make sense in context. Option D, *savvy*, means clever; someone can be savvy but still be honest.

32. A: *Incite* means to "urge" or "encourage." *Insight* is "the ability to see an underlying truth."

33. A: To *know* means to "have knowledge" of something. *No* is used to show dissent or denial.

34. B: *Steal* means to "take another's property without permission." *Steel* is a type of metal.

35. A: To *pare* down means to *reduce*. *Pair* describes a set of two things.

Spelling

36. A: Option A, *adversarial*, is spelled correctly.

37. D: Option D, *germane*, is spelled correctly.

38. B: Option B, *palpable*, is spelled correctly.

39. C: Option C, *subpoena*, is spelled correctly.

40. D: Option D, *suspicious*, is spelled correctly.

41. C: Option C, *facilitate*, is spelled correctly.

42. A: Option A, *interrogated*, is spelled correctly.

43. B: Option B, *independent*, is spelled correctly.

44. A: Option A, *heinous*, is spelled correctly.

45. D: Option D, *incorrigible*, is spelled correctly.

46. B: Option B, *perfunctory*, is spelled correctly.

47. A: Option A, *seditious*, is spelled correctly.

48. B: Option B, *surveillance*, is spelled correctly.

49. A: Option A, *tenacious*, is spelled correctly.

50. D: Option D, *vagrancy*, is spelled correctly.

Reading Comprehension

1. B: The author's main point is that witnesses can be unreliable. In paragraph 1, the author states that "the information officers receive is often inaccurate either because the individual was mistaken in his or her perception, was biased, or was purposefully deceptive." The other options are *reasons* witnesses can be unreliable.

2. A: The passage implies that officers must diligently investigate due to witness unreliability. The author states in paragraph 1 that officers "must rely on... statements from witnesses and involved parties... to draw conclusions about what actually occurred" during a crime, making Option B incorrect. Option C is incorrect because that passage states in paragraph 2 that "[t]he most frequent type of unreliable information is mistaken perception," not individual bias. Finally, in paragraph 5, the author states, "It is the officer's duty to use critical thinking, deduction, and logical reasoning to determine what is or is not reliable and why," so Option D cannot be correct; some witnesses can be determined to be reliable.

3. D: Dishonesty, mistaken perception, and bias are all mentioned in the passage as problems with witness reliability.

4. B: In paragraph 3, the author writes, "[w]hile some people have biases they are aware of, sometimes people have biases they are unaware of for a number of reasons." People are generally unaware of the bias they hold. The other options are untrue.

5. C: Paragraph 2 describes auditory occlusion as "a temporary loss or lessening of hearing; sounds are muted or unheard." While auditory occlusion is a sort of sensory disturbance, Option C is better than Option D because it offers a more precise definition. Option A is incorrect because auditory occlusion is not a *total* loss of hearing, just a temporary loss or lessening of hearing. It is not associated with vision, making Option B incorrect.

6. C: *Anomaly* means *abnormality*. In the passage, a *time anomaly* is an abnormality in experiencing time. A *commonality* is a shared trait, implying the opposite of *anomaly* in this context, making option A incorrect. Options B and D, *ambivalence* and *uncertainty*, have similar meanings and do not make sense here.

7. B: *Blatant* means *flagrant*. Option A, *obvious*, is close in meaning but is not the best answer, because it lacks the negative connotation of *flagrant*. Options C and D, *subtle* and *implied*, are oppositional in meaning to *flagrant*.

8. B: The overall point of the passage is that ranchers still suffer from cattle rustling. The passage addresses the issues of cost, meat certifications, and branding, but these are not the main ideas of the passage.

9. C: The rancher lost $100,000. Multiply 100 cows by $1,000 per cow: $100 \times 1000 = \$100,000$.

10. B: According to the passage, "CHP grades livestock on a step level from 1 to 5, with 1 being the lowest and 5 being the highest. The higher the meat's rating, the more natural, healthy, and flavorful it is, allowing the farmer to command a premium price."

11. C: The passage says that a higher rating from the CHP results in a higher price for meat; the CHP recommends against branding. Therefore, Option C is the best answer. In paragraph 4 it is stated that CHP claims "that branding animals is not humane." It can be inferred from this statement that branding hurts the animals, making Option A incorrect. In paragraph 3, the author writes, "[a]s farmers desire to return to natural and humane ways of farming and cattle raising, while also increasing their earnings potential, fewer farmers are branding their cattle." Clearly, branding *is* a major issue for ranchers, and it is unlikely that most ranchers brand their cattle in this climate, making Options B and D incorrect.

12. D: Paragraph 1 mentions the points made in Options A, B, and C. The passage never discusses services to help addicts overcome addiction.

13. B: *Diligently* means *persistently*. Options A and C, *neglectful* and *unconcerned*, do not make sense; ranchers and law enforcement are clearly attentive and concerned about this issue. Option D, *carefully*, has a slightly different meaning.

14. A: In paragraph 2, the passage states that "[t]he problem for ranchers... is that it's fairly easy to avoid detection while selling stolen livestock at auction. Why? The cows often are not branded." However, paragraph 3 discusses how higher ratings from the Certified Humane Project (CHP) mean meat fetches higher prices at market, and in paragraph 4 the author writes, "ranchers have a decision to make—protect the herd with brands or resist branding to achieve higher CHP step ratings." The passage never mentions addicts being members of the community, making Option B incorrect. It explicitly states that branding reduces the value of meat because it results in a lower rating from the CHP, making Option C incorrect. Finally, the CHP is presented as a partner, not an adversary, making Option D incorrect.

15. D: The main point of the passage is to stimulate thought. It presents a difficult issue: prisoner release. It also addresses two perspectives, noting that "[s]ome people believe a person who has committed a crime is lost and can never be redeemed," while "[o]thers believe there are justifiable reasons why any given crime was committed, and thus very few people should go to jail or prison for extended times." The passage also asks the reader to consider how to support prisoners in the community. Option B is incorrect because the passage does more than simply provide information—it poses questions in paragraph 2. Options A and C are incorrect because the passage is objective in its presentation of information and opinion. It never chooses a perspective.

16. B: Option B best addresses the ideas of the passage, which discusses the details of re-entry programs. The passage discusses multiple perspectives, making Option A incorrect. Option C is incorrect because the passage does not mention how to decrease recidivism. Option D is not the best option because it is too vague.

17. C: Option C is the best option since the passage discusses the value of collaboration among community stakeholders. Options A and B are differing opinions explicitly stated in the passage. Option D is an oversimplification; the author states that "[r]e-entry programs have shown success in many communities" but that "the perceived level of success may be well above or well below expectations."

18. D: Natural inclination. Options A, B, and C are incorrect because each can be a natural inclination.

19. A: Paragraph 2 provokes the reader into thinking more deeply about prisoner reentry by asking direct questions, illustrating the depth of the issue. The author does not provide an example or supporting details, making Options B and D incorrect. The point of paragraph 2 is not avoidance but provocation, making Option C incorrect.

20. C: To *redeem* means to "buy back," "recover," "exchange," or "reform." In this context, *redeemed* means "reformed."

21. B: Option B is correct because the passage clearly states that more than two-thirds of the 5.4 million individuals under adult correctional supervision are supervised in the community, either on probation or parole. This makes community supervision the majority of correctional oversight in the US. Option A is incorrect because community supervision is not rare; it is the most common form of correctional supervision. Option C is wrong because the passage does not mention whether the percentage has increased in recent years. Option D is also incorrect since the passage states more persons were on probation or parole than were incarcerated.

22. C: Option C is correct because the statistics show that most adults under correctional supervision in the US are managed in the community rather than incarcerated. Option A is incorrect because it falsely emphasizes incarceration, whereas the passage states that most adults under supervision are supervised in the community. Option B is incorrect because the passage does not state or imply that probation and parole are becoming less common. Option D is incorrect because the passage does not address historical trends or changes over time.

23. B: The passage presents a general overview of its topic, and then it uses statistical evidence, such as population percentages and exact figures, to support the presented viewpoint. Option A is incorrect because the passage does not compare opposing viewpoints. Option C is incorrect because there is no chronological narrative or sequence of events. Option D is incorrect because the passage does not present a problem or suggest any solutions.

24. C: The word *competent* is the key word for this claim, since *competent* is a judgment on the part of the writer. Option A is incorrect because it provides a factual definition—not a claim—of the adult correctional system. Option B is incorrect because it presents a specific numerical estimate rather than an assertion. Option D is incorrect because it gives a statistical ratio, not a claim or interpretive statement.

Practice Test #3

Writing

Clarity

Directions: In the following sentence pairs, identify the sentence that is most clearly written.

1.
   A) The engineer examined the blueprint, identifying potential flaws in the design that could affect structural integrity.
   B) The engineer reviewed the blueprint, recognized flaws, and even identified suggestions, so they may affect structural integrity.

2.
   A) Focusing on critical times in history, the primary source documents were clearly related to each other by the historian.
   B) The historian analyzed the primary sources, drawing connections between the events and their broader political implications.

3.
   A) The marketing strategy focused on targeting specific demographics, ensuring that all campaigns were aligned with market trends.
   B) The marketing plan aimed at specific demographics and focused on impactful trends aligned with all campaigns.

4.
   A) The architect drafted a building plan with green features for the future, though the environmental benefits were clearly outlined and prioritized.
   B) The architect designed a sustainable building using renewable materials, ensuring minimal environmental impact throughout the structure's lifespan.

5.
   A) The financial analyst reviewed the investment portfolio, identifying key areas for risk mitigation, but forgot to recommend strategies for improvement.
   B) The financial analyst reviewed the portfolio and suggested changes and therefore identified key areas to specify how those adjustments would reduce risk.

6.
   A) The lawyer drafted the contract carefully, addressing all potential legal concerns to protect the interests of both parties involved.
   B) The lawyer entirely designed the contract, addressing interests to both parties involved with potential legal concerns.

7.
  A) The teacher made suggestions about the thesis, she also explained about clarity issues, and the paper was considered shallow.
  B) The teacher's feedback clearly explained how the thesis could be improved for clarity and depth.

8.
  A) The developers stated that the software failed during testing due to a lack of necessary security updates.
  B) The developers failed the software because it lacked necessary security vulnerabilities and updates.

9.
  A) The nutritionist assisted her clients by structuring a meal plan better to improve energy and deeply sleep.
  B) The nutritionist designed a meal plan for her clients that better balanced protein, fiber, and nutrients.

10.
  A) The hikers crossed the ridge early to avoid uncharacteristically high winds predicted for the afternoon.
  B) Hiking early across the ridge, the hikers avoided predicted high winds for the afternoon.

11.
  A) The speaker engaged the audience before presenting key findings from the year-long study.
  B) After introducing the topic, the speech about the year-long study was initiated, and the results were discussed with the audience.

12.
  A) The technician shut down the machine before inspecting the malfunctioning control panel.
  B) Before inspecting the issue, which was quite difficult, the technician found and shut down the malfunctioning control panel.

13.
  A) The editor didn't accept the article; it had problems, and he was insistent on rejecting them.
  B) The editor rejected the article due to factual inaccuracies and inconsistent sourcing.

14.
  A) Simulated job interviews assist candidates in practicing questions under pressure.
  B) Designed to improve pressure, the interview candidate is assisted by simulated job interviews.

15.
  A) A meeting was held by the team after the product release to evaluate the data and determine what needed to be improved.
  B) The team met after the product release to evaluate what worked and what needed improvement.

16.
  A) The chef threw out the dish after realizing that it had spoiled overnight.
  B) Overnight, the chef found the dish was spoiled, so they discarded it.

17.

A) To enhance the song's depth and its texture, the recording musician used multiple layered tracks.
B) The musician used layered tracks during the recording to enhance the song's depth and texture.

18.

A) The marketing team responded to customer feedback and updated the campaign strategy.
B) The marketing team's email campaign and feedback trail updated the campaign strategy.

Vocabulary

Directions: Choose the word that is closest in meaning to the underlined word in the following sentences.

19. After a lengthy pursuit, the officer finally <u>apprehended</u> the criminal.

A) released
B) captured
C) questioned
D) observed

20. The detective was known for being exceptionally <u>meticulous</u> when analyzing crime scene evidence.

A) careless
B) thorough
C) clumsy
D) vague

21. The suspect's cooperation with investigators was <u>ephemeral</u>, ending as soon as he hired an attorney.

A) lasting
B) intense
C) stable
D) brief

22. New surveillance footage helped <u>vindicate</u> the officer by showing he had followed proper protocol.

A) accuse
C) pardon
C) defend
D) abandon

23. The judge questioned whether the photo had real <u>evidentiary</u> relevance to the case.

A) random
C) harmful
C) artistic
D) supportive

24. The judge found there was <u>probable</u> cause to issue the search warrant.

A) unlikely
C) no
C) likely
D) certain

25. The detective used an investigative approach to gather facts and uncover the truth.
   A) curious
   B) suspicious
   C) exploratory
   D) defensive

26. The report included quantitative data to support the officer's findings.
   A) emotional
   B) measurable
   C) unmeasurable
   D) vague

27. The court granted an expungement of the arrest record, erasing it from public view.
   A) exposure
   B) filing
   D) punishment
   D) deletion

28. Officers may enter without a warrant under exigent circumstances that involve immediate danger.
   A) urgent
   B) optional
   C) avoidable
   D) relaxed

29. The negotiator remained diplomatic to defuse tension between the suspect and the officers.
   A) rude
   B) persuasive
   C) tactful
   D) careless

30. The body camera footage was ancillary support for the officer's testimony.
   A) main
   B) opposing
   C) misleading
   D) additional

31. The court ordered the documents to be turned over forthwith.
   A) tomorrow
   B) eventually
   C) urgently
   D) later

32. The officer received a formal admonishment for failing to follow procedure.
   A) promotion
   B) praise
   C) warning
   D) explanation

33. The sergeant gave a lucid explanation of the legal procedures officers must follow during an arrest.
A) obscure
B) clear
C) dull
D) ambitious

34. The officer's altruistic decision to mentor at-risk youth showed a deep commitment to community service.
A) selfish
B) indifferent
C) hesitant
D) generous

35. The defendant remained obstinate during questioning, refusing to change his story under pressure.
A) flexible
B) kind
C) stubborn
D) passive

36. The prosecutor took a pragmatic approach by offering a plea deal to avoid a lengthy trial.
A) idealistic
B) realistic
C) emotional
D) abstract

Spelling

Directions: Read the following sentences and choose the correct spelling of the missing word.

37. The suspect had been under constant ______ due to suspicious activity.
A) survalence
B) surveillance
C) surveilence
D) survaliance

38. The court issued a ______ requiring the witness to appear and testify.
A) subpeona
B) supena
C) subpoena
D) subpena

39. There was ______ cause to search the suspect's vehicle based on the report.
A) probly
B) problable
C) probable
D) probebly

40. Officers responded quickly to the reported ______ at the intersection.
   A) incident
   B) incidant
   C) insident
   D) incedent

41. The crime scene was examined by a trained ________ expert.
   A) forrensic
   B) forensic
   C) forensick
   D) forensik

42. The ______ gave orders to the squad during the operation.
   A) leftenant
   B) leutenant
   C) lieutenant
   D) luitenant

43. The suspect was charged with the illegal ______ of a firearm.
   A) possession
   B) posession
   C) possesion
   D) possesstion

44. The ______ fled the scene before officers arrived.
   A) assailent
   B) assailant
   C) assalent
   D) asailant

45. The department focuses on tracking down dealers of illegal ______.
   A) narcatics
   B) narcotiks
   C) narkotics
   D) narcotics

46. The driver was clearly ______ when he failed the field sobriety test.
   A) intoxikated
   B) intoxicated
   C) intoxicateded
   D) entoxicated

47. The officer had no ______ to pursue the suspect into another county.
   A) juristiction
   B) jurisdiction
   C) jurisidiction
   D) jurisdictian

48. The quick ______ of the fugitive prevented further harm.
A) apprehesion
B) apprihension
C) apprahension
D) apprehension

49. The suspect was arrested for ______ on private property.
A) trespasing
B) trespassingg
C) tresspassing
D) trespassing

50. The trunk was found to contain illegal ______ and contraband.
A) wepponary
B) weaponry
C) weaponery
D) weponary

51. The case was ruled a ______ after evidence confirmed intentional killing.
A) homacide
B) homicide
C) homiciede
D) hommicide

52. Officers collected ______ from the crime scene, including fingerprints.
A) evedince
B) evidance
C) evadince
D) evidence

53. The suspect's ______ lasted several hours before release on bail.
A) detainmant
B) detanement
C) detainement
D) detainment

54. The defendant was found guilty of a ______ and fined $500.
A) misdemeanor
B) misdimenor
C) misdameanor
D) missdemeanor

Reading Comprehension

Passage One

The Americans with Disabilities Act (ADA) and Section 504 prohibit discrimination against individuals on the basis of disability (42 U.S.C. § 12131, et seq. and 29 U.S.C. § 794). These laws protect all people with disabilities in the United States. An individual should be considered to have a "disability" if he or she has a physical or mental impairment that substantially limits one or more major life activities, has a record of such an impairment, or is regarded as having such an impairment. Examples include attention-deficit/hyperactivity disorder (ADHD), autism spectrum disorder (ASD), chronic illnesses like diabetes or asthma, learning disabilities like dyslexia, vision or hearing impairments, and mental health conditions like anxiety or depression.

1. What is the main purpose of the ADA and Section 504?
   A) to provide financial support for individuals with disabilities
   B) to prohibit discrimination against individuals with disabilities
   C) to define what constitutes a disability under federal law
   D) to raise awareness about mental health conditions

2. Which of the following can be inferred from the passage?
   A) Disabilities are only recognized if they are physical in nature.
   B) Mental health conditions are not considered disabilities under the ADA and Section 504.
   C) Only people with visible disabilities are protected by these laws.
   D) The laws protect individuals with both physical and mental disabilities.

3. Which sentence in the passage represents a claim about who is considered to have a disability?
   A) "The Americans with Disabilities Act (ADA) and Section 504 prohibit discrimination against individuals on the basis of disability."
   B) "An individual should be considered to have a 'disability' if he or she has a physical or mental impairment that substantially limits one or more major life activities."
   C) "Examples include attention-deficit/hyperactivity disorder (ADHD), autism spectrum disorder (ASD), chronic illnesses like diabetes or asthma, learning disabilities like dyslexia, vision or hearing impairments, and mental health conditions like anxiety or depression."
   D) "These laws protect all people with disabilities in the United States."

4. What is the main focus of the passage?
   A) the challenges faced by individuals with mental health conditions
   B) the various types of disabilities and their impacts on life activities
   C) the historical development of the ADA
   D) the legal protections under federal law for individuals with disabilities

5. What is the significance of the examples listed in the passage (e.g., ADHD, ASD, chronic illnesses)?
   A) They illustrate types of disabilities that are not covered by the ADA and Section 504.
   B) They demonstrate the broad range of conditions that qualify as disabilities under these laws.
   C) They highlight the most common disabilities in the United States.
   D) They show the mental health conditions that are excluded from legal protection.

6. According to the passage, which scenario could still result in ADA protection, even if no formal diagnosis exists?
   A) experiencing short-term fatigue after physical activity
   B) recovering from an illness such as the flu
   C) being treated as though one has a significant impairment
   D) lacking stable employment due to external factors

Passage Two

When a person tries to buy a firearm, the seller, known as a Federal Firearms Licensee (FFL), contacts the National Instant Criminal Background Check System (NICS) by phone. The prospective buyer fills out the Alcohol, Tobacco, and Firearms (ATF) form, and the FFL relays that information to the NICS. The NICS staff performs a background check on the buyer. That background check verifies that the buyer does not have a criminal record or isn't otherwise ineligible to purchase or own a firearm. Since the system was launched in 1998, more than 500 million checks have been done, leading to more than 2 million denials. The FBI provides full service to the FFLs in thirty-one states, and the other states complete their own checks.

7. What is the main purpose of the NICS?
   A) to record firearm purchases
   B) to contact FFLs
   C) to issue firearm licenses
   D) to verify buyer eligibility

8. Which of the following inferences can be made from the passage?
   A) The NICS check is mandatory for all firearm purchases.
   B) The NICS has been operational since 1998.
   C) FFLs are responsible for performing background checks.
   D) The FBI handles all background checks.

9. What is the main purpose of the passage?
   A) The history of firearm regulation
   B) The role of the FBI in law enforcement
   C) The legal requirements for owning a firearm
   D) The process of purchasing a firearm

10. Which sentence presents a claim?
    A) The NICS performs a background check.
    B) More than 500 million checks have been done.
    C) The FBI provides full service to thirty-one states.
    D) NICS checks help prevent ineligible firearm purchases.

11. What is the significance of the 500 million checks mentioned in the passage?
    A) It reflects the number of firearms sold.
    B) It shows the NICS' operational efficiency.
    C) It highlights the number of firearm licenses issued.
    D) It indicates the number of firearm-related crimes.

12. What can be concluded about the role of the FFL in the background check process?
A) The FFL is responsible for contacting the NICS and relaying buyer information.
B) The FFL directly conducts the background checks on firearm buyers.
C) The FFL only verifies the criminal history of the buyer.
D) The FFL processes all firearm sales without involving the NICS.

Passage Three

The law 34 U.S.C. § 12601 prohibits state or local law enforcement officers from acting corruptly and repeatedly engaging in conduct that violates the constitutional rights of individuals. This law makes it unlawful for state or local law enforcement officers to engage in a pattern or practice of conduct that deprives persons of rights protected by the Constitution or laws of the United States. The types of conduct covered by this law can include, among other things, excessive force, discriminatory harassment, false arrests, coercive sexual conduct, and unlawful stops, searches, or arrests. To be covered by this law, the misconduct must constitute a "pattern or practice"—it cannot simply be an isolated incident.

13. Which of the following best summarizes the main purpose of 34 U.S.C. § 12601?
A) to protect individuals from one-time violations of their constitutional rights by law enforcement officers
B) to prevent state and local law enforcement officers from engaging in patterns of misconduct that violate constitutional rights
C) to grant state and local law enforcement officers the authority to conduct searches and arrests
D) to establish the procedures for filing complaints against law enforcement officers

14. What is the effect of the law described in the passage on state and local law enforcement?
A) It allows law enforcement officers to engage in isolated incidents of misconduct.
B) It mandates that law enforcement officers can be disciplined only for criminal acts.
C) It prohibits law enforcement officers from participating in patterns of unconstitutional behavior.
D) It establishes the rules for lawful searches, arrests, and stops.

15. Which of the following is an example of conduct that would be covered by 34 U.S.C. § 12601?
A) a single officer using excessive force in a particular situation
B) a law enforcement officer following all legal procedures in an arrest
C) a law enforcement officer arresting someone without probable cause during a one-time incident
D) law enforcement officers repeatedly engaging in discriminatory harassment or false arrests

16. Based on the passage, which of the following would most likely not be a violation under 34 U.S.C. § 12601?
A) a department regularly conducting unlawful searches without warrants
B) an officer engaging in excessive force as part of a recurring practice
C) a one-time unlawful arrest by an officer acting alone
D) a police agency consistently targeting individuals based on race during stops

17. Which sentence in the passage makes a claim about the scope of 34 U.S.C. § 12601?

A) "The law 34 U.S.C. § 12601 prohibits state or local law enforcement officers from acting corrupt and repeatedly engaging in conduct that violates the constitutional rights of individuals."

B) "To be covered by this law, the misconduct must constitute a 'pattern or practice'—it may not simply be an isolated incident."

C) "The types of conduct covered by this law can include, among other things, excessive force, discriminatory harassment, false arrests, coercive sexual conduct, and unlawful stops, searches, or arrests."

D) "This law makes it unlawful for state or local law enforcement officers to engage in a pattern or practice of conduct that deprives persons of rights protected by the Constitution or laws of the United States."

18. Which one of the following best explains why the phrase "pattern or practice" is emphasized in the passage?

A) to clarify that all forms of police misconduct, regardless of frequency, are prosecutable under the statute

B) to distinguish between systemic violations and one-time actions by individual officers

C) to suggest that isolated incidents are more difficult to detect and prove in court

D) to show that the law primarily targets federal law enforcement agencies rather than state or local ones

Passage Four

As a means to strengthen communities' abilities to address youth gangs and provide law enforcement with specialized training for countering street gang crime, in October 2009, the National Youth Gang Center (NYGC) merged with the National Gang Center (NGC). This unification signified a recognition that dangerous street gang activities transcend the ages of the members and that a balanced, comprehensive approach is needed to reduce gang involvement and levels of gang crime. Consolidation of the centers has leveraged resources and resulted in a single, more efficient entity responsive to the needs of criminal and juvenile justice professionals, law enforcement, youth- and community-serving practitioners, researchers, and the public.

19. What is the primary purpose of the passage?

A) to describe a shift in how gang crimes are punished

B) to promote a new youth outreach program

C) to argue that gang crime is primarily an adult issue

D) to explain the merger of two gang-related centers and its impact

20. What can be inferred about the relationship between youth and adult gang activity?

A) Youth gang crime is more dangerous than adult gang crime.

B) Gang activity often overlaps between youth and adults.

C) Youth are not involved in serious gang crime.

D) Adult gang members were the only concern of the NGC.

21. Which one of the following sentences related to the passage is a claim?
   A) "In October 2009, the National Youth Gang Center (NYGC) merged with the National Gang Center (NGC)."
   B) "This unification signified a recognition that dangerous street gang activities transcend the ages of the members."
   C) "The NYGC was established to provide training for police departments."
   D) "Researchers have long studied gang behavior in communities."

22. How is the passage structured?
   A) It presents a chronological narrative followed by a personal opinion.
   B) It contrasts two opposing views about gang prevention.
   C) It lists unrelated facts about gang crime.
   D) It describes a change and explains the reasoning and results.

23. What does the author suggest is the benefit of the centers' consolidation?
   A) It reduced the overall crime rate in major cities.
   B) It removed overlap in law enforcement agencies.
   C) It provided a more unified, efficient response to gang crime.
   D) It ended all distinctions between youth and adult gang members.

24. What does the paragraph imply is necessary to reduce gang crime?
   A) increased federal funding for schools
   B) fewer police in high-crime areas
   C) longer sentencing for gang members
   D) addressing multiple factors that contribute to the problem

Answer Explanations #3

Writing

Clarity

1. A: The sentence is clear, grammatically sound, and professionally structured. It uses precise language such as "closely examined" and "potential flaws . . . that could affect structural integrity." Option B is incorrect because it is unclear what "they" refers to, and the sentence has awkward phrasing, such as "identified suggestions."

2. B: This sentence effectively demonstrates how the historian "analyzed" sources and "drew connections" to broader implications. Option A is incorrect because the modifier "focusing on critical times in history" seems to describe "the primary source documents," not the historian, which creates a dangling effect.

3. A: The sentence is precise and clearly organized, using professional terminology like "targeting specific demographics" and "aligned with market trends." It uses proper grammar. Option B is incorrect because it is awkwardly constructed with phrases like "aimed at" that detract from the message's clarity.

4. B: The sentence clearly states that the architect used renewable materials in the design and directly links them to "minimal environmental impact." Option A is incorrect because of vague phrases ("green features for the future") and a confusing clause structure ("though the environmental benefits were clearly outlined or prioritized") that undermine clarity.

5. A: This sentence effectively explains what the financial analyst did and did not do. Option B is incorrect due to its confusing structure, including an awkward use of the word *therefore*. This confusing logic weakens the overall message.

6. A: This sentence demonstrates a complete legal action by specifying that the contract addressed "all potential legal concerns," while Option B shifts the phrase "potential legal concerns" to be a part of "both parties involved" and uses awkward phrasing like "entirely designed."

7. B: The sentence is grammatically clear and concise, with the teacher's feedback clearly explained as focused on improvement for clarity and depth. Option A, however, is incorrect because it is a run-on sentence and lacks coherence. It combines several points into one sentence without proper punctuation or structure.

8. B: The sentence clearly says what the developers did and why. Option B notes that the software "lacked necessary security vulnerabilities," which does not make sense.

9. B: The sentence is clear and precise and correctly uses the concept of balancing nutrients ("protein, fiber, and nutrients"). This formulation clearly conveys what the nutritionist did to design a meal plan. Option A, however, contains awkward phrasing ("a meal plan better to improve energy and deeply sleep").

10. A: The sentence is clear and grammatically correct. It concisely explains that the hikers crossed the ridge early to avoid predicted winds. Option B, however, contains awkward phrasing like "hiking early across the ridge."

11. A: The sentence is clear and grammatically correct. It accurately presents the logical flow of the speaker's actions: engaging the audience before presenting key findings. Option B uses the passive voice and an awkward structure.

12. A: The sentence is clear and structured properly. It accurately describes the technician's actions of shutting down the machine before inspecting the malfunction. Option B, however, is incorrect because, while it contains much the same information, it is not structured in a clear and concise manner.

13. B: The sentence is grammatically correct and clearly explains the editor's reasoning for rejecting the article. "Factual inaccuracies and inconsistent sourcing" are specifically mentioned, providing precise feedback. Option A states the same general information but lacks readability and coherence.

14. A: The sentence is clear and uses straightforward language to describe the function of simulated job interviews in helping candidates practice under pressure. Option B, however, is incorrect because it uses passive voice, uses the awkward phrase "Designed to improve pressure," and misplaces this modifier before "the interview candidate."

15. B: The sentence is grammatically correct and clearly conveys the purpose of the meeting ("evaluate what worked and what needed improvement"). It is concise and focuses on key information. Option A, however, is incorrect because it uses passive voice and is less concise.

16. A: The sentence is clear, concise, and grammatically correct. It explains that the chef discarded the dish after realizing it had spoiled. Option B, however, is incorrect because it implies the chef noticed the spoilage overnight, while the first sentence makes it clear that the food had spoiled overnight.

17. B: The sentence is clearly written and effectively communicates the musician's intentional use of layered tracks to enhance the song's depth and texture. It uses professional language and maintains a logical structure. Option A is incorrect because it adds unnecessary words.

18. A: The sentence is clear and grammatically correct. It describes the marketing team's actions in response to customer feedback. Option B, however, implies that it was the "email campaign and feedback trail" that updated the campaign strategy.

Vocabulary

19. B: *Apprehended* means captured. Option A is incorrect because *released* means let go of. Option C is incorrect because *questioned* means asked questions, expecting answers. Option D is incorrect because *observed* means looked at carefully.

20. B: *Meticulous* means thorough or showing great attention to detail. Option A is incorrect because *careless* means lacking attention or precision. Option C is incorrect because *clumsy* means awkward or uncoordinated. Option D is incorrect because *vague* means unclear or not specific.

21. D: *Ephemeral* means brief or lasting for a short time. Option A is incorrect because *lasting* suggests permanence. Option B is incorrect because *intense* refers to strength, not duration. Option C is incorrect because *stable* implies steadiness or consistency over time.

22. C: *Vindicate* means to defend or clear someone of blame. Option A is incorrect because *accuse* means to allege wrongdoing. Option B is incorrect because *pardon* means to forgive, typically in legal terms, which is more intense than defending. Option D is incorrect because *abandon* means leave without support.

23. D: *Evidentiary* relates to supportive value in proving something in court. Option A is incorrect because *random* suggests lack of relevance. Option B is incorrect because *harmful* is unrelated to evidentiary value. Option C is incorrect because *artistic* relates to creative expression, not legal standards.

24. C: *Probable* cause refers to something being likely or reasonably believed. Option A is incorrect because *unlikely* implies uncertainty, which is the opposite of *likely*. Option B is incorrect because "no cause" would mean a lack of justification. Option D is incorrect because *certain* implies a greater degree of proof than is implied by *probable*.

25. C: *Investigative* means exploratory, focused on uncovering facts or details. Option A is incorrect because *curious* describes a personality trait, not a method or approach. Option B is incorrect because *suspicious* implies doubt rather than inquiry. Option D is incorrect because *defensive* implies protection, not investigation.

26. B: *Quantitative* means measurable and relates to data expressed in numbers. Option A is incorrect because *emotional* data would be subjective. Option C is incorrect because *unmeasurable* suggests the opposite of *quantitative*. Option D is incorrect because *vague* lacks precision, the opposite of quantitative.

27. D: *Expungement* means deletion of a record from public view. Option A is incorrect because *exposure* suggests making something public. Option B is incorrect because *filing* means submitting or recording something. Option C is incorrect because *punishment* is the consequence of a crime, not its erasure.

28. A: *Exigent* means urgent, justifying immediate action such as entering without a warrant. Option B is incorrect because *optional* implies a choice, not necessity. Option C is incorrect because *avoidable* suggests the opposite of urgency. Option D is incorrect because *relaxed* implies calm, not emergency.

29. C: *Diplomatic* means tactful, especially in sensitive or tense situations. Option A is incorrect because *rude* is inconsiderate, not diplomatic. Option B is incorrect because *persuasive* refers to convincing others, not necessarily showing tact. Option D is incorrect because *careless* lacks the thoughtfulness needed in diplomacy.

30. D: *Ancillary* means additional or providing supplementary support. Option A is incorrect because *main* is the primary, not the supporting, element. Option B is incorrect because *opposing* suggests contradiction. Option C is incorrect because *misleading* implies inaccuracy or deception.

31. C: *Forthwith* means urgently or without delay. Option A is incorrect because *tomorrow* could imply waiting. Option B is incorrect because *eventually* suggests a delayed timeline. Option D is incorrect because *later* also implies non-immediacy.

32. C: *Admonishment* means a warning or formal reprimand. Option A is incorrect because *promotion* is a reward. Option B is incorrect because *praise* is positive feedback. Option D is incorrect because *explanation* provides reasoning, not discipline.

33. B: *Lucid* means clear, especially in explanations or thinking. Option A is incorrect because *obscure* means unclear or hard to understand. Option C is incorrect because *dull* means boring, not clear. Option D is incorrect because *ambitious* implies high expectations.

34. D: *Altruistic* means generous or selflessly concerned for others. Option A is incorrect because *selfish* is the opposite. Option B is incorrect because *indifferent* means lacking concern. Option C is incorrect because *hesitant* implies uncertainty.

35. C: *Obstinate* means stubborn, especially in refusing to change one's mind. Option A is incorrect because *flexible* implies willingness to adapt. Option B is incorrect because *kind* refers to being nice, not persistence. Option D is incorrect because *passive* implies inactivity, not firm resistance.

36. B: *Pragmatic* means realistic, focusing on practical results. Option A is incorrect because *idealistic* means guided by ideals rather than practicality. Option C is incorrect because *emotional* decisions are based on feelings, not strategy. Option D is incorrect because *abstract* ideas are theoretical, not grounded in reality.

Spelling

37. B: Surveillance is the correct spelling.

38. C: Subpoena is the correct spelling.

39. C: Probable is the correct spelling.

40. A: Incident is the correct spelling.

41. B: Forensic is the correct spelling.

42. C: Lieutenant is the correct spelling.

43. A: Possession is the correct spelling.

44. B: Assailant is the correct spelling.

45. D: Narcotics is the correct spelling.

46. B: Intoxicated is the correct spelling.

47. B: Jurisdiction is the correct spelling.

48. D: Apprehension is the correct spelling.

49. D: Trespassing is the correct spelling.

50. B: Weaponry is the correct spelling.

51. B: Homicide is the correct spelling.

52. D: Evidence is the correct spelling.

53. D: Detainment is the correct spelling.

54. A: Misdemeanor is the correct spelling.

Reading Comprehension

1. B: The main purpose of the ADA and Section 504 is to prohibit discrimination against individuals with disabilities. This is stated directly in the passage. Option A is incorrect because the laws focus on equal rights, not financial support. Option C is incorrect because, although the laws do define disability, their primary purpose is to prevent discrimination. Option D is incorrect because raising awareness is a possible effect but not the central purpose of the laws.

2. D: The passage explicitly states that the ADA and Section 504 protect individuals with both physical and mental impairments. This supports the inference that the laws apply to both types of disabilities. Option A is incorrect because it wrongly limits the scope of the laws to physical disabilities. Option B is false because mental health conditions are listed as protected. Option C is incorrect because visible disabilities are not the only ones covered. Additional disabilities covered are nonvisible conditions like anxiety and learning disorders.

3. B: The sentence "An individual should be considered to have a 'disability' if he or she has a physical or mental impairment that substantially limits one or more major life activities" presents a claim defining who "should" qualify as having a disability under the law; this is true regardless of the fact that these are the traits that do define who is considered to have a disability. Options A, C, and D provide examples or consequences of the definition but do not directly define it.

4. D: The main focus of the passage is explaining the legal protections for individuals with disabilities under federal law, specifically the ADA and Section 504. Option A narrows the focus too much to mental health, which is only part of the broader discussion. Option B describes part of the content, but it is not the central focus. Option C is incorrect because the historical development of the ADA is not discussed.

5. B: The examples of ADHD, ASD, and others demonstrate the wide range of conditions that qualify as disabilities under the ADA and Section 504. Option A is incorrect because these conditions are covered by the laws. Option C is inaccurate because the passage does not state that these are the most common disabilities. Option D is incorrect because mental health conditions are explicitly included, not excluded.

6. C: The passage notes that a person may be protected under the ADA and Section 504 even if they are "regarded as" having an impairment. This means a person can receive protection based on how they are perceived, even without a formal diagnosis. Options A and B describe short-term or minor conditions that do not substantially limit life activities. Option D is incorrect because employment instability due to general, external (non-disability-related) factors does not trigger protection under the laws.

7. D: The NICS exists to verify whether a prospective firearm buyer is eligible to own or purchase a firearm. Option A is incorrect because its primary function is eligibility verification, not recordkeeping. Option B is incorrect because the NICS is contacted by FFLs, not designed to contact them. Option C is incorrect because the NICS does not issue licenses.

8. B: The passage states that "the system was launched in 1998," which supports this inference. Option A is incorrect because the passage does not confirm that all firearm purchases require a NICS check. Option C is wrong because FFLs submit information; they don't conduct the checks themselves. Option D is inaccurate because only thirty-one states receive full service from the FBI, while others perform their own checks.

9. D: The passage describes the steps in the firearm purchase process, emphasizing the background check system. Option A is inaccurate, as the passage does not provide a historical overview. Option B is too broad and not the central focus. Option C is incorrect because it doesn't explain legal ownership requirements, just the background check process.

10. D: "NICS checks help prevent ineligible firearm purchases" is a claim because it interprets the outcome or purpose of the checks, rather than stating a verifiable fact. Options A, B, and C are factual statements directly supported by the passage and do not express a viewpoint or judgment.

11. B: The reference to 500 million checks illustrates how extensively the NICS has been used, supporting its operational effectiveness and reach. Option A is incorrect because the checks are not the same as firearm sales. Option C is wrong because the NICS doesn't issue licenses. Option D is incorrect because the passage makes no link to firearm-related crimes.

12. A: The FFL's role is to contact the NICS and provide buyer information for the background check, as explained in the passage. Option B is incorrect because FFLs do not conduct the checks themselves. Option C is incorrect because FFLs do not verify criminal histories. Option D is incorrect because FFLs must involve the NICS in the process.

13. B: The law prohibits patterns or practices by state or local law enforcement that violate constitutional rights. Option A is incorrect because one-time violations are not covered. Option C is wrong because the law limits, rather than grants, authority. Option D is incorrect, as the law focuses on misconduct, not complaint procedures.

14. C: The passage explicitly states that the law prevents law enforcement from engaging in patterns of unconstitutional behavior. Option A is incorrect because, although this law doesn't pertain to isolated incidents, it does not permit them. Option B is incorrect because discipline is not limited to criminal acts. Option D is inaccurate because setting rules for lawful procedures is not the focus.

15. D: Repeated conduct such as discriminatory harassment or false arrests constitutes a pattern of misconduct, which is covered under the law. Options A and C involve isolated incidents, which are not addressed by this statute. Option B describes lawful behavior and is not a violation.

16. C: A one-time unlawful arrest by an officer is not considered a pattern or practice and therefore does not fall under this law. Options A, B, and D describe repeated or systemic misconduct, which the law aims to prevent.

17. A: This is correct because of the key word *corrupt*, which is an opinion. Options B, C, and D elaborate on the scope or consequences but are not as clear or primary in describing the law's coverage.

72. B: Emphasizing "pattern or practice" highlights that the law addresses systemic misconduct rather than isolated incidents. Option A is incorrect because not all forms of misconduct are covered; only those that are repeated are considered in a pattern. Option C is unrelated to the law's emphasis. Option D is wrong because the law targets state and local law enforcement, not federal agencies.

18. D: The passage explains the merger of two gang prevention centers and the resulting benefits. This is its main purpose. Option A is incorrect because the passage does not discuss punishments. Option B is wrong because the passage is not about outreach promotion. Option C misrepresents the author's viewpoint.

19. B: This statement is supported by the passage, which says that "dangerous street gang activities transcend the ages of the members." Options A, C, and D are not supported by any text in the passage.

20. B: This is a claim because it presents an interpretation of the gangs as "dangerous," which is an opinion. Option A is a factual statement describing an event that occurred at a specific time. Option C is also a factual statement describing the purpose of the NYGC, not an interpretation or opinion. Option D is incorrect because it states an observable fact and does not argue or assert a particular viewpoint.

21. D: The passage first describes a change (the merger) and then explains the reasoning and outcomes. Option A is incorrect because there is no personal opinion. Option B is incorrect because no opposing views are presented. Option C is incorrect because the facts are related and support a central point.

22. C: The author states that the consolidation created a single, more efficient entity responsive to multiple groups, showing the benefit of unification. Option A is incorrect because crime rates are not mentioned. Option B is not supported by the text. Option D is incorrect because the distinction between youth and adult gang members is still acknowledged.

23. D: The passage refers to the need for a "balanced, comprehensive approach," implying that effective gang crime reduction requires addressing multiple factors. Options A, B, and C are not mentioned or are contrary to the approach suggested in the text.

Appendix

A

ABDICATE (verb): to relinquish authority or responsibility

ABERRANT (adj.): in an abnormal state

ABIDE (verb): to accept or act in accordance with (a rule, decision, or recommendation)

ABJECT (adj.): low, miserable

ABOLISH (verb): to formally end something, like a law

ABRIDGE (verb): to shorten

ACCOLADE (noun): an award, honor, or acknowledgement

ACCOMPLICE (noun): someone who has helped another person commit a crime

ACCORD (noun): agreement, harmony

ACQUIESCE (verb): to give in or submit

ACUMEN (noun): sound mental judgment

ADVERSARY (noun): opponent

AFFABLE (adj.): friendly; outgoing

AFFECT (verb): to act on; to produce an effect or change in

ALIENATE (verb): to make hostile or indifferent

ALLEGATION (noun): a formal accusation against somebody

ALLEVIATE (verb): to relieve or ease

ALOOF (adj.): distant

AMASS (verb): to collect or gather

AMBIGUOUS (adj.): having more than one meaning or interpretation

AMBIVALENCE (noun): mixed feelings or contradictory attitudes

AMBULATORY (adj.): able to walk; related to walking

ANTAGONIZE (verb): provoke; oppose

APATHY (noun): indifference or lack of emotion

ASSAILANT (noun): one who performs a physical attack

ASSAULT (verb): to physically attack

ASSIGNMENT (noun): a given task, duty, or job

AUGMENT (verb): to increase

B

BELIE (verb): to give an inaccurate impression of; to contradict

BELITTLE (verb): to make someone or something seem unimportant; to denigrate

BELLIGERENCE (noun): aggressive behavior

BENIGN (adj.): not harmful

BIZARRE (adj.): strange; unusual

BLATANT (adj.): obvious

BREVITY (noun): concise speech or writing

C

CAJOLE (verb): to coax or persuade with flattery

CALLOUS (adj.): emotionally hardened

CANDID (adj.): honest

CAPITULATE (verb): to surrender, usually under agreed conditions

CENSURE (noun): condemnation or disapproval, usually formal

CLEMENCY (noun): mercy

COALESCE (verb): to combine into a whole

COERCE (verb): to force by using pressure, intimidation, or threats

COLLUSION (noun): secret agreement or cooperation

COMMISSION (noun): the act of commit- ting; carrying out an action

COMPLACENT (adj.): self-satisfied

COMPLIANT (adj.): obeying, yielding

CONFIDE (verb): to entrust information privately

CONFOUND (verb): to confuse

CONSPIRACY (noun): a secret plot or plan

CONTAMINANT (noun): an impurity

CONTEMPT (noun): disrespect, especially in a court of law

CONTROVERSIAL (adj.): given to debate or argument

CONVERGE (verb): to come together

COPIOUS (adj.): plentiful; abundant

CORROBORATE (verb): to support

CORRUPT (verb): (adj.) to be dishonest or immoral in action

COUNTERFEIT (noun): not genuine

CREDENCE (noun): acceptance as true

CRYPTIC (adj.): secret; mysterious

CURSORY (adj.): hasty

D

DEBILITATE (verb): make weak

DELINQUENCY (noun): actions outside of the law, especially of minors; an overdue debt

DELUSION (noun): irrational belief not rooted in reality

DEPLETE (verb): to use up

DERELICT (adj.): abandoned or neglected, especially property

DETAIN (verb): deprive of freedom

DEVIATE (verb): to depart from the norm

DISCREPANCY (noun): a disagreement between facts

DISDAIN (noun): scorn; contempt

DISINGENUOUS (adj.): dishonest

DOCILE (adj.): manageable; submissive

DUBIOUS (adj.): suspect

E

EDICT (noun): command; proclamation

EFFECT (noun): (of a law) having legal validity

ENCUMBER (verb): to burden

ENTAIL (verb): to involve

EQUILIBRIUM (noun): balance

EQUIVOCATE (verb): to deceive by using ambiguous language

EVANESCENT (adj.): disappearing quickly

EXACERBATE (verb): to make worse

EXCLUSIONARY (adj.): characterized by excluding something

EXCULPATE (verb): to clear from guilt

EXONERATE (verb): pronounce not guilty of criminal charges

EXPEDITE (verb): to hasten or accelerate

EXPENDABLE (adj.): unnecessary; disposable

F

FACILITATE (verb): to make possible; to make easier

FLOURISH (verb): to thrive

FORFEITURE (noun): loss, usually for legal reasons

FOSTER (verb): help develop, help grow

FRANTIC (adj.): emotionally out of control

FRAUD (noun): an act of criminal deceit

FRAUDULENT (adj.): involving criminal deceit

FURTIVE (adj.): cautious; secretive

FUTILE (adj.): unsuccessful

G

GARNER (verb): to gather

GERMANE (adj.): relevant

GLEAN (verb): to collect; to obtain

GRIEVANCE (noun): a cause for complaint

GUARANTEE (noun): promise, especially of repair or replacement for a product

GUILE (noun): cunning

H

HARASSMENT (noun): aggressive intimidation

HEINOUS (adj.): very wicked; offensive; hateful

HINDER (verb): to delay or obstruct

HONE (verb): sharpen

HYPOCRITICAL (adj.): professing feelings or virtues one does not have

I

IMMUNITY (noun): being invulnerable to something

IMPRESSION (noun): a feeling or understanding resulting from an experience

IMPRISON (verb): to confine

INCITE (verb): to stir up

INCONSPICUOUS (adj.): not noticeable

INCORRIGIBLE (adj.): not able to be corrected

INCRIMINATING (adj.): charging or suggestive of guilt or blame

INDICTMENT (noun): a formal statement by an attorney and jury charging an individual with an offense

INITIATIVE (noun): the first of a series of actions

INNOCUOUS (adj.): harmless

INTEGRITY (noun): moral value

IRREFUTABLE (adj.): unable to be denied

J

JEOPARDIZE (verb): to threaten with loss or failure

JUDICIAL (noun): of or relating to a court

JUDICIARY (noun): judges; judicial authority

JUDICIOUS (adj.): having good judgment

JURISDICTION (noun): authority, especially to make legal judgments

JUVENILE (adj.): of or relating to minors or young people

L

LEGITIMATE (adj.): lawful

LENIENCY (noun): mercifulness; acquiescing to someone's wishes

LICENSE (noun): freedom to act; a document granting the ability to perform an action or occupation

LISTLESS (adj.): lack of energy

LUCID (adj.): clear

M

MAINTAIN (verb): to enable to continue

MAYHEM (noun): deliberate injury of someone; a state of violent chaos

MISCREANT (noun): one who breaks the law

MITIGATE (verb): to alleviate

MORBID (adj.): marked by an unhealthy interest in death

MUNDANE (adj.): ordinary, often boring

MYRIAD (noun): a large indefinite number; (adj.): uncountable

N

NARCISSISTIC (adj.): having an inflated idea of one's own importance

NEBULOUS (adj.): undefined in content, form, or limits

NEFARIOUS (adj.): wicked or evil

NEGLIGENT (adj.): characterized by neglect and undue lack of concern

NEGLIGIBLE (adj.): insignificant

NEXUS (noun): a connection

NONCHALANT (adj.): casually unconcerned

NUISANCE (noun): a bother or annoyance

NULLIFY (verb): to void, especially legally

O

OBLIVION (noun): unconsciousness; a state of being unaware

OBSCURE (verb): to make it difficult to see something; (adj.): unclear; esoteric

ONUS (noun): a burden or difficult concern

P

PACIFY (verb): to appease

PALPABLE (adj.): able to be felt

PEJORATIVE (adj.): derogatory; demeaning

PERFUNCTORY (adj.): routine

PERIPHERAL (adj.): on or to the side

PETULANT (adj.): rude

PILFER (verb): to steal

PLACATE (verb): to soothe

PRECEDENT (noun): an event occurring earlier that sets an example

PREVALENT (adj.): widespread

PREVARICATE (verb): to lie; to equivocate

PROCLIVITY (noun): a natural inclination

PROFUSE (adj.): abundant

PROVISION (noun): supplying or providing something; an item that provides sustenance (like food)

PROVOKE (verb): to instigate

PROXIMITY (noun): closeness

Q

QUEASY (adj.): nauseous

QUELL (verb): to calm; pacify; to put an end to; to allay or quiet

QUIRK (noun): an odd trait or behavior

R

RECALCITRANT (adj.): uncooperative

RECANT (verb): to take back; disavow one's opinion or belief

RECIPROCAL (adj.): shared by two parties

RECLUSIVE (adj.): isolated

REDRESS (noun): compensation for wrong-doing

REFUTE (verb): to disprove; to successfully argue against

REPEAL (verb): to revoke; to annul

REPLETE (adj.): full of something

REPROBATE (noun): depraved, unprincipled, wicked person

RESCIND (verb): to cancel

RESOLUTE (adj.): determined

RESPITE (noun): an interval of rest

S

SABOTAGE (verb): to destroy intentionally

SANCTION (verb): give authority or permission to

SAVVY (adj.): shrewd

SCRUTINIZE (verb): to look at closely

SEDITIOUS (adj.): inciting rebellion

SOVEREIGN (noun): high authority, such as a monarch; independent

SPECULATION (noun): reflection on a subject

STATUTE (noun): an act passed by a legislative body

STRINGENT (adj.): demanding strict attention to rules and procedures

SUBDUE (verb): to bring into control

SUBTLE (adj.): delicate; not strong or over-bearing

SUCCINCT (adj.): concise

SUPPRESS (verb): to subdue, especially by force

SURVEILLANCE (verb): to secretly watch or supervise

T

TANTAMOUNT (adj.): the same as

TENACIOUS (adj.): persistent; determined

TENUOUS (adj.): weak

THWART (verb): to defeat

TRANQUIL (adj.): calm; content

TRANSIENT (noun): a vagrant; a person without a permanent domicile

U

USURP (verb): to seize

V

VAGRANCY (noun): being without any obvious means of support or livelihood

VERBOSE (adj.): wordy

VILIFY (verb): to denounce; to slander

W

WARRANT (noun): a legal document authorizing police to take an action such as making an arrest

WARY (adj.): cautious; untrusting

WILLFUL (adj.): oppositional; purposeful

Z

ZEAL (noun): excessive enthusiasm

ZEALOT (noun): an excessively enthusiastic person, especially regarding religion

Dear PELLET B Test Taker,

Great job completing this study guide! The hard work and effort you put into your test preparation will help you succeed on your upcoming PELLETB exam. Thank you for letting us be a part of your educational journey.

We have other study guides and products that you may find useful. Search for us on Amazon.com or let us know what you are looking for. We offer a wide variety of study guides that cover a multitude of subjects.

If you would like to share your success stories with us, or if you have a suggestion, comment, or concern, please send us an email at support@triviumtestprep.com.

Thanks again for choosing us!

Happy Testing,
Trivium Test Prep Team

Made in the USA
Coppell, TX
06 August 2025

52827715R00070